THE PAPYRUS BASKET:
The School in the Wilderness

OVER 200,000 COPIES SOLD

Phyllis Young-Ae Kim
Winner of the Christian Publishing Cultural Award in Korea

"This book is a <u>must read</u> for all who are looking for an example of God at work today through the lives of the faithful."
— President Alvin O. Austin, Ph.D.,
LeTourneau University, Longview, Texas

The Papyrus Basket: The School in the Wilderness
by Phyllis Young-Ae Kim

Printed in the United States of America

ISBN 1-60034-339-2

Unless otherwise indicated, Bible quotations are taken from the HOLY BIBLE, NEW INTERNATIONAL VERSION®. Copyright © 1973,1978,1984 by International Bible Society.

Handong Global University(HGU) is an Affiliate Institution of the Council for Christian College & University(CCCU) headquartered on Capitol Hill in Washington, D. C. (www.cccu.org)

Handong Global University: www.handong.edu
The Office of the President: ygkim@handong.edu
Papyrus Basket Membership: gxlove@handong.edu, lahandong@hotmail.com

Author Contact : youngae8357@daum.net

www.xulonpress.com

RECOMMENDATIONS

"When former world renowned NASA scientist and professor Young-Gil Kim left his prestigious professorship at the Korea Advanced Institute of Science and Technology (KAIST) to join the newly established Handong Global University to raise up future global Christian leaders, and when Mrs. Young-Ae Kim started to write a private testimony, God transformed the private testimony into the public testimony named Papyrus Basket, which would move the hearts of millions"

Rev. Billy Jang-Whan Kim,
Former President of Baptist World Alliance,
and President of Far East Broadcast Company,
Seoul, Korea

"Handong Global University is indeed God's University which consists of obedient and dedicated Christian professors called by Him. Through prayers, Handong has been able to educate and send out competent and honest global Christian leaders despite the various perils, difficulties, and hardships that existed from the start"

David Yonggi Cho,
Senior Pastor of Yoido Full Gospel Church,
Seoul, Korea

"I first met President Young-Gil Kim and his wife Young-Ae Kim when they visited the LeTourneau University campus several years ago and I became intrigued by their vision for Handong Global University. I caught a glimpse of the story of struggle and sacrifice that they and Handong had endured since its founding in 1995. Later, after visiting the campus in Pohang, Korea, I became deeply immersed in the faith journey of Handong, and these two Christian leaders and the students they serve. But it was only after reading *The Papyrus Basket: The School in the Wilderness,* that I became fully engaged in the most intriguing story. Young-Gil and Young-Ae have been led and upheld by God through some of the most amazing experiences and challenges that Christian leaders can face. This book is a <u>must read</u> for all who are looking for an example of God at work today through the lives of the faithful"

Dr. Alvin O. Austin, President,
LeTourneau University,
Longview, Texas U.S.A.

"From the moment I opened this book, I could not put it down for the next 10 hours and in order to wipe the overflowing tears, I found myself constantly reaching for a tissue box. It amazed me that I still had the capacity to shed these warm tears. I do not think Mrs. Young-Ae Kim intended this book to make people cry, but I wondered why I could not stop these tears"

Rev. HanHum Oak,
Founding Pastor of Sarang Community Church,
Seoul, Korea

ACKNOWLEDGEMENTS

For the publication of this book Papyrus Basket, in English, I have received heartfelt encouragements and invaluable helps from many devoted, loving Christian brothers and sisters, as well as pastors in Korea and abroad. Especially, I would like to express my deepest gratitude to Christine Jae-Hee Kim who, after three days of fasting and prayers, decided to undertake the difficult task of translating this book into English. Despite her busy business commitment as a successful executive of a corporation, she diligently labored for months in providing the first English draft translation of the original Korean text, which provided the foundations for this edition. I also wish to thank Sun-Hee Kim for giving her undivided attention while writing this book in Korean originally. Furthermore, I would like to express my thanks to Professors Gihong Kim and Hayne Shin of Handong Global University for their spending much time and effort on the editing of the text. My deep appreciations are also extended to Mrs. Juanita Buzzard and Susan Wittman, the wives of Dean Lynn Buzzard and Professor Mike Wittman of Handong International Law School, for their helpful suggestions.

My special word of thanks is also given to the President and Mrs. Gaylen Byker of Calvin College, Grand Rapids, Michigan, and to the President and Mrs. Alvin Austin of LeTourneau University, Longview, Texas, for their consolation and comfort while my husband was imprisoned in 2001.

Finally, I would like to thank my beloved husband, Young-Gil for his endless prayers and encouragements he has given to me whenever I encountered impassable obstacles and impediments and was about to lose my grip of the rope which I was clinging on.

"Praise and glory and wisdom and thanks and honor and power and strength be to our God for ever and ever. Amen!"- Revelations 7:12

Phyllis Young-Ae Kim
Pohang, Korea

Table of Contents

PREFACE

"Let me tell you what He has done for me" (Psalm 66:16).

*T*his is the story of a miraculous drama played on the twenty-first century stage at Handong Global University (HGU), a newly created Christian University in Korea – in which God has been the master director. Since Handong Global University opened its doors in 1995, God has brought swift and vast progress, even through numerous impediments and adversity. From the outset, God has called my husband as his instrument and as the president of HGU which became more evident as the time passed. This is my humble attempt to inscribe as a witness some of the wondrous things God has accomplished through Handong and to testify miracles I have seen as the wife of the president. I wish I could find more words in English to better capture and describe His workings and blessings at Handong.

I married an atheistic scientist who was born and educated in a strict Confucian family in a conservative rural area of Korea. It was during our marriage, in 1974 when he was working at NASA in Cleveland, Ohio, that my husband became a born-again Christian. Then, some 20 years later, in 1994, he was called upon by God to lead a newly established Christian University of Handong Global University in Pohang, Korea. Since his marriage with me through the tenure at HGU, I witnessed his transformation into a devout Christian. I was right with him as he painstakingly went through the hardheaded quest of intellectual application of scientific reasoning to eventually discover the Truth in the Bible and evidences of faith.

Even before Handong opened, the school faced serious financial difficulty, and it made our life unfold in completely unexpected and unplanned ways. When we first realized the difficulty, we naively hoped that the circumstances would improve somehow as time passed. However, as we moved forward, we found our path becoming even darker and narrower. As our suffering and fears intensified, we shook in fear. Because human beings by nature have learned to live self-reliantly, all who are called by God experience unique training while He acts to disarm and overhaul them.

As I look back, I cannot but believe that God purposefully subjected us to the painful and treacherous passage in our lives so that we may walk through times of thick fog. Who would have believed that a man God called to become a university president end up behind prison bars? The Lord led us to trust nothing else but His hands by taking away one by one all that we had been proud of and treasured, including our names, our self-respect, our reputations, our positions and our possessions. We shuddered from withdrawal symptoms each time one of these cords was cut. We were students in God's "desert school" and we have traveled to this day becoming broken and shattered along the path.

In desert school, God rescued the Israelites out of slavery in Egypt through many miracles, culminating in the crossing of the Red Sea. He promised to deliver them to a land flowing with milk and honey. But when the time came for the Israelites to fight and take possession of their Promised Land, they lost faith in God. Twelve leaders were sent out to spy out the land, and when they came back, ten predicted defeat for the Israelites because they lost faith and thought enemies appeared to be much stronger than them. God was angry with the Israelites and swore that not one man of that generation would enter the Promised Land but instead would wander through the desert for 40 years. Yet, even though the Israelites spent 40 years in the desert because of their rebellion against God, He led them throughout their entire journey, guiding and protecting them with pillars of fire and clouds and feeding them with manna from above.

"The LORD your God led you all the way in the desert these forty years, to humble you and to test you in order to know what was in your heart, whether or not you would keep his commands.

He humbled you, causing you to hunger and then feeding you with manna, which neither you nor your fathers had known, to teach you that man does not live on bread alone but on every word that comes from the mouth of the LORD. Your clothes did not wear out and your feet did not swell during these forty years. Know then in your heart that as a man disciplines his son, so the LORD your God disciplines you" (Deuteronomy 8:2-5). The desert was a place of uncertainty and nothingness from a worldly perspective, but God led the Israelites through the desert to mold them so that they might come to know Him. And as the Israelites traveled through this desert, God provided for every one of their needs. He put the Israelites through the desert school.

We could not foresee even a single day ahead, but I knew that our path was the safest path. I witnessed countless times how God was present at every turn, and I came to profess out loud that those who leave on a journey led by God's hands are traveling along the safest path no matter how dark the road may seem. As I experienced our God who never took His eyes off from us even for a moment, I could only exclaim, "God is awesome! He truly lives!" As I recorded the stories of how God walked alongside Handong over the past ten years, there were times when I was angry at God, and there were times when I shed tears of thanksgiving. Just like friends who become closer as they experience all kinds of triumphs and tragedies together, I became closer to Jesus, day by day.

The primary force behind my testimony is the word of God. If I had not held on to His words through daily meditation of the Bible, I would not have made it to this day. The words of the Bible were not mere letters printed on paper. His word was power! Suffering and darkness were opportunities for finding the true treasure (Isaiah 45:3). *"The fear of the Lord is the key to this treasure"* **(Isaiah 33:6).**

As I applied God's word to our circumstances, I came to realize that God's people in all generations are subjected to the similar training based on the same formula, for which only the inputs vary depending on the individual circumstances. Hence, I believe that our story of following the path unseen belongs to all believers. As a witness of the living God who fills every corner of Handong, I want to share our story so that everything - our mistakes, our failures, our fears, our pains, and even the smallest of our hurts - may be used for His glory. As I write our story, I am fearful that this book may elevate my husband in some way. If there is any part of the book guilty of such offense, I ask for your understanding that it comes only from a wife's love for her husband. My husband and I wish with all our hearts that only our living God be magnified through this book, which is my only purpose for writing it.

This is not the finished story of Handong by any means. It is merely the first book of testimony of Almighty God's power and presence through the founding phase of Handong. Those who have been a part of Handong from the beginning probably have many testimonies of their own. We do not yet know what God will do through Handong based on this foundation. What excites us the most is that students not only from Korea but also from all over the world, especially from Afghanistan, Albania, Brazil, Bulgaria, Burundi, Cambodia, Cameroon, Haiti, Hungary, Ghana, India, Indonesia, Israel, Jordan, Malaysia, Mongolia, Pakistan, Russia, Saudi Arabia, South Africa, Swaziland, Thailand, Tunisia, Uganda, Uzbekistan, and other nations (so far 58 nations), are coming to Handong. We cannot yet know what God intends to do by bringing these young people from across the globe to the remote city of Pohang in Korea, but our hearts are excited when we envision our students growing up to be leaders of their own home countries. However, what is certain is that God's amazing story of Handong will continue to unfold and that "The Books of the Acts of Handong" will continue to be written. I am thankful that I am allowed to be the first torch bearer of record-keeping task as the wife of the founding President.

Summer 2005 in Pohang, Korea, where the "The Books of the Acts of Handong" continue to be written,

Phyllis Young-Ae Kim

PROLOGUE

The Unforgettable Day

May 11, 2001!! It was the day of sentencing for my husband Young-Gil's trial. Young-Gil had been accused by the prosecutor's office of improprieties involving the school's finances. That morning, as before, I stayed behind at home rather than see Young-Gil stand in court. As I walked with him to the front door, I said,

"Our God, the Righteous Judge, will be with you today."

I thought that the trials, which had taken place over the past nine months, would finally end on that day. The sentencing should have begun at 9:30 am, but even past 11 am, no news came to me at home. As time passed, I started to feel anxious. Then the phone rang. It was my son Jimmy Ho-Min in Seoul.

"Mom, the verdict isn't good."

He took a deep breath and continued. "Dad got a prison sentence of two years, and the Vice President got a year and a half. They were arrested in court."

"Arrested in court? What do you mean?"

"They were taken directly to prison from the court."

His voice was shaking. The school staff must have contacted my son in Seoul first because they could not bear to tell me the terrible news directly themselves. I fell to the floor. I felt like falling into a deep abyss. *"Save me, O God, for the waters have come up to my neck. I sink in the miry depths, where there is no foothold. I have come into the deep waters; the floods engulf me" (Psalm 69:1-2).*

I heard that many students, their parents, alumni, professors, and staff had gathered in court to view the trial. When the two defendants walked into the courtroom, the audience began to stir and make noise. The judge entered soon thereafter. The room instantly fell into a tense silence. Before reading the sentence, the judge said, "Neither side should create any disturbance regarding the sentence. This case will surely go to the Supreme Court regardless of today's verdict, so any disturbances will only be disadvantageous to your side in the future."

Everyone paid absolute attention to every word that the judge uttered as he read the sentence.

"The defendants avoided court appearances on numerous occasions, and due to their frequent trips abroad without an obvious purpose, there is a risk that they may escape abroad or destroy evidence. Due to the malicious intent of their crimes, the court sentences the President and the Vice President to two years in prison and one-year-and-six-months in prison respectively, and the court orders their immediate detention!"

The courtroom fell deadly silent. Those in attendance were shocked by the unexpected result. They were frozen to their seats for a long time. But I was told that there were some who were delighted with the sentencing, raising their fists and shouting songs of victory.

"Awake, and rise to my defense! Contend for me, my God and Lord. Vindicate me in your righteousness, O Lord my God; do not let them gloat over me" (Psalm 35:23-24).

Starting at noon, TV stations started spreading the news throughout the country. Newspapers printed headlines that read, "President Young-Gil Kim of Handong Global University and its Vice President Arrested in Court today on Charges related to the School's Finances!"

Since the school opened, Young-Gil had been through many tribulations as he had been summoned around 80 times to the court, the prosecutor's office, and the union office. But this case seemed much more ominous than all the previous ones. The school's administration was even paralyzed for a while as accounting records were seized for the prosecution's investigation.

On some days, Young-Gil returned home at midnight from an arraignment after being questioned for 14 hours. He sat in his study, completely exhausted and staring blankly into space. How could even I, his wife, understand his sufferings!

One day, Young-Gil was dictating a response to a letter of complaint that had been submitted to the Ministry of Education. As he listed all the unbelievable events of the past, one by one, his heart became heavy and he let out a deep groan. But even that was only for an instant – he gathered his thoughts and continued his work.

When the prosecution's charges were made, my husband made his final pleading:

"Before Handong opened, the founder's business had an industrial accident and could no longer contribute financially to the school. In the midst of such circumstances, Handong opened, and I could not leave the school when professors from both within and outside of Korea as well as students from all over the country came to Handong with their trust in me as their first President. I endured countless difficulties as I held onto my mission of educating future leaders. As the President, my first priority had been normalizing school affairs, and there have been unintentional mistakes along the way. Everything was the result of my inexperience with administrative matters, and I have inconvenienced many people and caused hardships."

Don't Consider Yourself Wronged

In the evening, I received a call from the wife of a Handong professor.

"Mrs. Kim, I'm envious of President Kim. Not everyone gets to go to prison under such circumstances. How many people in our times have been sent to prison while doing God's work? God trusts President Kim to the point of sending him to prison. People like us couldn't go even if we wanted to. I'm so proud that my husband works with President Kim at Handong. Mrs. Kim! Don't ever be discouraged or sad. If you are, God may feel disappointed. God is the living God! There are many people who are praying for President Kim and you.

"Mrs. Kim, do not be shaken by people's compliments or criticism. The only one on whom we can depend, the only one who can encourage us, is God Almighty. Don't feel like you've been wronged in any way. Jesus must be even more outraged than we are.

Since what has happened exceeds all common sense, surely God must have allowed it to happen. While I was praying for you, God reminded me of Isaiah 51:12-16 which I want to share with you now. ...*I, even I, am he who comforts you......* Mrs. Kim, God will soon bring President Kim out of prison, and from then on, Handong will no longer lack bread"

Then I suddenly remembered a passage from the Scripture: *"For I know the plans I have for you, declares the Lord, plans to prosper you and not to harm you, plans to give you hope and a future" (Jeremiah 29:11).*

The First Visit

The next day, I visited the prison to see my husband. With my heart pounding, I awaited my turn. *"You understand, O Lord; remember me and care for me. Avenge me on my persecutors. You are long-suffering – do not take me away; think of how I suffer reproach for your sake" (Jeremiah 15:15).* A few minutes later, the prisoner No. 433 and 443 were called over the speakers. Young-Gil's number was 433, and Vice President's number was 443. I could barely calm my heart and walk across the courtyard with several professors to the visiting room. Young-Gil came in following a guard, and he sat in a very small space across a clear plastic divider. He was a completely different person from the one who had left home the day before. He was wearing a yellowed, shabby prison uniform with a number tag on his chest, his face puffy from lack of sleep and without his eye glasses.

"President Kim!"

The professors who had accompanied me could not say a word. My husband spoke very emotionally. "Everyone, please don't worry. I'm fine. I have good cellmates, and I don't have to do clean-up duty, or fold the blankets...." This was the man who, as late as yesterday, was excitedly discussing the school's visions and dreams! My heart sank.

"But, I need to get out soon. The school needs $1 million this month."

He was still full of worries about money.

"Young-Gil, don't worry. The money has been taken care of. Early this morning, Pastor Ha called me and said that there was an emergency elders' meeting at the church. They decided to donate $1 million that the school needs this month."

As soon as he heard me saying that, his face brightened like a child's. He spoke as if he had come to visit a neighbor's house.

"Oh, really? Then I can stay here a while longer." He relaxed.

"Young-Gil, don't think about money any more and get some rest here. God is working even harder since you cannot do anything. There are quite a few people who are envious of you, saying that not everyone can come to a place like this even if they wanted to. They envy you because you came here while doing God's work. Now that our children are both married and have their own lives, let's just think about how to please God for the rest of our lives."

"I agree with you. *"All things will work toward good for those who love God and have been called according to His purpose" (Romans 8:28)*. I've been so busy until now, and I want to meet with God intimately while I'm in here. Please tell all the students not to be distressed and rather to focus only on their studies. And since they don't allow metal-frame glasses in prison, get me ones with a plastic frame."

Only then did I understand why he was not wearing his glasses. My heart ached when I realized that I did not even know his eye prescription. I did not even have an extra pair of glasses for him. What an unprepared wife I was.

I also met Vice President in the next room. I called him out with a lump in my throat.

"Don't worry, Mrs. Kim. My cellmates are nice to me, and they don't assign clean-up duties to me since I'm the oldest. I cannot see President Kim since we are considered conspirators. The red mark on my number tag signifies 'conspiracy.'"

As I left the two of them behind in prison, tears began to flow down on my cheek uncontrollably. On the way home, the driver who had been with Young-Gil for the past six years began to pour out his heart as well.

"Yesterday since President and Vice President disappeared behind the court gate, I drove back to school feeling the burden of his empty seat. He'd stood before the court so many times, but I'd always brought him home. I cannot believe what has happened. Yesterday, I couldn't drive because of all the tears in my eyes. Who knows better than me all that the President had to go through these past several years! Accusations followed accusations, and the Ministry of Education kept asking for reports. He had to prepare for trial, appear before the court and the prosecutors, and take care of school business during the day, while speaking at fundraising engagements in the evening. Who knew all that he had to do in a day!

He usually had two speaking engagements in a week, and he had to gather supporters for the Papyrus Basket at the same time. On some Sundays, he had three speaking engagements. After an all-day session at the prosecutors' office, he would speak in the evening with power as if nothing had happened in the day time, and I used to wonder how he could do that. There were times when I couldn't even encourage him to eat dinner because I didn't think he would have any appetite under the circumstances. Just standing beside him, I couldn't help but cry and feel faint.

Between speaking engagements, the back seat used to be filled with the school's promotional materials with barely enough space for him to sit. There were many times when he didn't even have time to eat. Sometimes he would run to a hamburger place and bring back something quick to eat in the car.

One year, on a bitterly cold Sunday evening, we went to a church which invited him to give testimony. The church was located on the top of a hill, and as the road had turned icy, the car couldn't climb up the hill. The President and I had to get out of the car and start climbing up the hill carrying boxes full of promotional materials for the school and the Papyrus Basket subscription forms. But the road was so slippery, and we fell and the boxes slid down the road. We grabbed them and climbed back up, only to fall down again. There were days like that.

One day, we were in the southern part of Korea. When the President began to speak, the professor who had accompanied us and I quietly slipped out of the building. We could not distribute the Papyrus Basket brochures to the attendees without the church's approval, so we were always very careful to see how the church reacted. So, we sat outside under a street light and started inserting the Papyrus Basket flyers to each school catalog. All of a sudden, a gust of bitter winter wind blew and sent the flyers flying all over the street. We ran after them trying to catch as many them as we could."

If it had not been for the grace of God, how could Young-Gil have endured all those incidents? Who could deny that we have managed to come this far only because of the new strength that God gave us? I remembered each days of our past as if they had all taken place today.

PART I: VISION

CHAPTER 1:

Honoring the Commission to Rebuild

A Phone Call

On January 20, 1994, we were in our apartment at the Faculty Housing of the Korea Advanced Institute of Science and Technology (KAIST). After dinner, my husband Young-Gil and I sat down with a cup of tea, our first in a long while. A bitter winter wind was hitting the windows outside, but we were enjoying a leisurely conversation in the coziness of our home. Then, all of sudden, the phone rang. It was Mr. J. Sohn, an attorney and friend of us for many years.

"Dr. Kim! A new university, called Handong, will be established based on Christian principles and will open next year in Pohang city. The founder, T.H. Song, was searching for a Christian scientist to lead the university, and he decided to invite you to become the founding president. I also recommended you as the ideal person for the position, given your academic credentials and your walk with God. Would you consider accepting the position?"

After listening to his friend, Young-Gil interrupted him and said, "I'm thankful and honored by your recommendation, but I'm not the right person for the position. As you know, I'm a research scientist and a professor. Even though I taught for the past 15 years, I have no prior experience in university administration."

My husband had a pained look on his face and hung up the phone with saying that he would pray about it.

"What did he say?" I asked.

"He said 'how could an elder say 'no' to such a request without even praying about it first?' His words pricked my heart."

My husband clearly looked disconcerted. As a man who openly professed Jesus Christ as his Lord and Savior, he might have realized that he had not yet completely surrendered the lordship over his life to Him.

From that day on, we began to pray with a heavy burden on our hearts.

"O Lord! Give us the wisdom to discern whether this is a call from you or from men."

We opened our ears to all channels of communication from God – through sermons, meditations on His word, and prayers. On the Sunday following the phone call, we listened to the sermon of our Pastor Yong-Jo Ha of Onnuri (All Nations) Presbyterian Church. It was on Acts 9.

"One day godly Ananias received a call from God to baptize Saul. At the time, Saul was infamous for persecuting Christians. Ananias could not understand the call, nonetheless, he reacted responsively to the voice of the Holy Spirit and obeyed. The great apostle Paul was born because of Ananias' immediate obedience. Even now, God is looking for those who will listen to His voice with a sensitive ear and obey. There are many Christian universities in the world, but there are only a few that profess Jesus Christ as the Lord of the university and its academics, where academia and faith are one. Our generation needs universities that are founded upon pure Christian faith."

What relation is there between Ananias' obedience and Christian universities? It was as if Pastor Ha were preaching with prior knowledge of our circumstances. We began to wonder if things were starting to move in a direction that we did not want.

A University Founded on a Vineyard

We received another call from Mr. Sohn. Unable to refuse his suggestion that we view the construction sites and meet the founder, Young-Gil got on a plane for Pohang city. As I saw him off, worries filled my heart. Being content with our current life, I was nervous that Young-Gil might end his life-long science research and start something new in which he had no experience. Certainly, it would be a risk with an unpredictable future. I could not let go of the thought that the title of professorship at KAIST was more fitting for my husband. But I was also afraid that my own thoughts might stand in the way of the work that God might have planned and commanded.

When Young-Gil returned, he had a lighter expression on his face.

"I met the founder. He looked like a modest man, and he has prepared about 200 acres of land for the campus site. He heads a medium-size company that is involved in industrial waste process and disposal business. He had a pure passion for a Christian-spirited university" he said brightly.

I interrupted, "But we don't know anything about him. Just looking at your elder brother (Dr. Ho-Gil Kim, the charter president of Pohang University of Science and Technology, POSTECH), you know how complicated and full of headaches it is to be a university president. It wouldn't be so bad if one of the largest conglomerates in Korea was the founder and backer, but this man heads only a midsize company. The future of the university will hang on how well his company does. Don't say yes just like that."

In January 1994, I accompanied my husband on his second trip to Pohang city. The way to the site passed the city of Pohang through a long, winding coastal road heading north. The blue ocean and its white waves filled my eyes. Pine trees lined along the road. It was a clear and sunny day, but the winter ocean wind was bitter. "How could there be a university in this desolate place?"

The car stopped after a long drive at a construction site where we could only see the sea, the hills, and the sky. The area administratively belongs to the city of Pohang, but it was five miles to the north of the city. A pine tree forest surrounded the place, and the bright rays of winter afternoon sun fell on the red clay. Newly planted grapevines looked like they could barely survive the harsh winter wind. A university constructed on a vineyard! *"I am the vine; you are the branches. If a man remains in me and I in him, he will bear much fruit; apart from me you can do nothing" (John 15:5).*

For a moment, I visualized new leaders of our generation pouring out of this place.

We climbed to the top of a building from where we could see the surroundings better. Across the rice field in front of the school was a small village. A lake fenced in by thick pine trees and hills, where rare cranes are said to roost, caught our sight. As if telling us to think of nothing else but studying, the place looked as peaceful as a monastery. I tottered in the ocean wind that was blowing. The serene surroundings and the gusty wind created a curious contrast.

The construction manager showed us the underground facilities where the utilities would be maintained, and the central power station where the automated power plant machinery would be housed. Our attention was drawn to the blueprint of the chapel that was to stand at the entrance. It seemed to proclaim that Handong Global University would be founded on Christian principles.

The Name of "Handong"

Young-Gil asked one of the starting members of the school, "Why did you name the school as 'Handong'? Isn't it better to have a name that better expresses the Christian spirit of the university?"

I too had been thinking that Handong ("Korea-East" in Chinese character) was too common a name.

"There is a story behind that," said one of the staff.

In order to get the city interested and involved, the founding committee held a contest to select a name for the school for a $1,000 prize. They received over 130 entries, from which they selected a few and brought them to the founder. Among the various names recommended, the founder chose the name "Handong," which was relatively low on the list. "Handong means the cradle of the academia, located at Korea-East." The name contained the hope that this school would be like the rising sun of the East and becomes a cradle of faith and academia for the young students in the 21st century. After selecting Handong as the school name, the committee contacted the winner. A child answered the phone and said that his parents were at church. The officer asked the child, "What does your father do?"

"He is a pastor," answered the child.

Pastor S. Woo had started a small Presbyterian church nearby. Desperately needing $1,000 for the church, he submitted an entry for the school name contest and was at his church that day praying for his entry to be selected.

It must have been the prayer of this pastor and his wife that a name near the bottom of the list caught the eye of the founder! God was involved with this school even from the very beginning! We were deeply moved. Handong was no longer a common name to us. Our hearts were beginning to change.

The founder was a self-made man who had established a business in industrial waste disposal after many years of hardship. When his business became successful, he looked for an opportunity to make a contribution to the society and he decided to establish a Christian-spirited university. We sensed his determination in his words:

"My faith is still weak, but I'm here today because of my wife's prayers. Many people have prayed for the founding of Handong. I would very much like to invite you, a man of God and a scientist, to become the first president of Handong. If you accept, it will be a great honor for us."

Young-Gil asked the founder, "Is it truly your decision to establish a new university based on pure Christian principles?"

The founder, with his eyes gleaming brightly, said, "Yes. It had been our goal from the very beginning to raise up such a university, and that is why we want to invite you. Dr. Kim! We will pour all our efforts into raising a great Christian university here. Please accept the post of the chartered university president!"

After listening to the founder, Young-Gil said, "Then I will hesitate no longer. It is an honor for me that you've called me to serve for this important work."

I looked at Young-Gil with a surprise. Even that very morning on our way to Handong, he had not yet made a decision. He had merely visited to see the construction site with me. In addition, we did not know anything about the school's situation!

I wondered how he could say "yes" without investigating further, but I knew my husband better than anyone else. He tended to look at the big picture, not the details.

That day, the founding committee reported to us that the school's finances were fairly stable compared with other private universities in Korea. In order to create a university of high caliber, it would be critical to have devoted Christian professors and staff, competent students, exceptional academic programs, and most importantly, the funds to support them all. Without the financial backing, all plans may end up as a dream. When we listened to the committee's financial plan, we began to believe in the stability of financial support to launch a fine university.

In spite of some misgivings, we slowly began to relax, and we started to plan the details of this new dream. But from that day on, our lives changed forever and became mired in endless worries and anxiety.

Go to the Land I Will Show You

A few days later, I went to the U.S. Embassy to run an errand for Young-Gil, who was scheduled to travel to the United States the next day for a science conference. But his visa was rejected due to some technical complications. I was at a loss, knowing that a delay in his travel would cause problems for the conference. There was nothing else to do but to wait through the weekend before he could travel. I was agitated since I was scheduled to travel with him, but he was quite calm.

He said, "There is nothing we can do. An impossible situation has occurred, and perhaps, that means that God has some other plan for us. Let's worship at our church tomorrow and then leave."

We would not have been able to attend the worship service had we left the day before. We sat in our usual seats up front and opened the church bulletin.

"God's Call and Obedience (Genesis 12:1-4)," the sermon title for the day, caught our attention. Why this particular topic? I felt that the title actually read, "God's Call to Handong Global University and Our Obedience." I carefully listened to the Pastor's sermon.

"God sometimes calls us to leave where we are today. The first reason is to teach us how to completely rely on God. Because where we are today is too comfortable, safe, and familiar to us, we do not rely on God for all things. The place to which God calls us to go is an unknown world, a place that we have never experienced before, a place that is unfamiliar to us. It is a place where there are worries, fears, and uncertainties. Perhaps famine, desperation, and persecution await us there. All knowledge and experiences that we have acquired and which we rely upon may become useless there. We may experience our complete and utter inability there. It is a place where we can only rely on God's word. That is why God calls us to leave."

I listened nervously, thinking of the comfortable research and teaching environment at Korea Advanced Institute of Science and Technology (KAIST), a tenured professorship, the exceptional students, and the relationships of respect and affection that last long after graduation. It was a life with a guaranteed future, a place of security and tranquility. What a challenge it would be for my husband to lead a university and be responsible for management rather than research. God knew better than anyone else that my husband spent most of his time working with instrument and not with people! On top of that, who could guarantee that a new university in rural area would have a rosy future? The pastor continued.

"The second reason for calling us to leave the place where we are is to teach us how to be free. We bind ourselves with too many chains of possessions, position, and pride. We will be able to learn true freedom in the new place. Furthermore, for those who have been called to leave, the place they are now may no longer be a place of security – because God is no longer there with them. The new place can be challenging and scary, but it is actually safer there – because God will be with them there.

"God promised to bless the man who obeyed and left his father's house to travel to a land unknown. He said, 'All people on earth will be blessed through you, and you will be a blessing.' The one thing that a person called to leave must remember is that we must follow only the word of God. Circumstances may change, but God's promise never changes!"

The message was a sound of thunder to us. I had remained nervous even after Young-Gil had tentatively agreed with the founder to accept the position. As if reprimanding me, God made me hear His voice that said, "Go to the place I have called you!"

Uncontrollable tears flowed down my face. Young-Gil also took the handkerchief from my hands.

"Lord, are you calling us now? How can you give such an overwhelming order to people like us? Lord! Are we truly hearing your voice?" I appealed to God.

We stood up after the service. Some friends who were sitting behind us must have noticed that something unusual was happening to us. They asked, "Is everything all right?"

How could we explain that we had to abandon the lives that we had lived up until this moment and depart on a new path?

Young-Gil said on our way home, "I now know why our travel plan was delayed. God wanted us to confirm the calling. If that is so, let's pack and move. We are God's soldiers, and we must please the One who has called us. Think of Elder S. Choe: He left a successful dental hospital to run a farm and spread the Gospel in China. Compared to him, we are far better off. What a worthy cause it is to train young students and to raise them as leaders who will change the world with the Gospel in one hand and professional knowledge in the other. If my research seems more important than God's command, then that has already become an idol for us." *"To man belong the plans of the heart, but from the Lord comes the reply of the tongue" (Proverbs 16:1).*

God Speaks to Us Once More

How fragile and conniving the human heart is! When I got home, the grace that I had experienced at church all but disappeared, and worries began to fill my heart thinking about the big adventure that we faced. "Things would be different if the school's foundation were backed by a major conglomerate..." This thought continued to weigh me down.

In 1979, when we were completing our 12 years of life in the United States to return to Korea, Young-Gil had hesitated in giving up scientific research in the States. But this time, I was the one who was hesitating. I wanted to avoid God's command, and I began to negotiate with God. I told Young-Gil.

"God spoke through yesterday's message in a general way. Wouldn't it be great if He spoke to us specifically one more time?

Even Gideon asked God to send the morning dew on a wool fleece and then asked Him to reconfirm by having it dried the next morning."

I was speaking as if God was not listening. But He must have heard my childish complaints. A few days later, God again gave us amazing words through the pastor.

"From now on, continue meditating on the book of Nehemiah. Like Nehemiah, you will fight spiritual battles of opposition and interference. God's precious leaders will pour out of Handong Global University and bear God's vision for our times in the 21st century. But this path is a path of tearful prayers on knees like the one that Nehemiah, one of our forefathers of faith, traveled on. Do not rely on men; rely only on God."

Although I could not shake a sense of foreboding in my heart, we could not escape God's call.

Nehemiah was taken captive to Persia and was living a life of comfort as the cupbearer to King Artaxerxes. One day, after hearing that the walls of Jerusalem were falling down and its gates burned with fire, he prayed with tears for his country.

Nehemiah reminded us of our own country. At the end of the nineteenth century, Korea had an unpredictable future amidst power struggles among the strongest countries. However, in 1880s, God stepped in and the Gospel was proclaimed to our people through foreign missionaries. He allowed us to receive salvation and the Holy Spirit through blue-eyed missionaries, many of whom became martyrs. He led us to pray through the 36 years of Japanese occupation, and He repaid our 36 years of wandering through the desert by granting independence to our nation.

However, we sinned against God as we fought and killed each other during the tragedy of the Korean War in 1950-53. Our Lord rescued us again from dire poverty and restored us to achieve the miracle of Han River. However, we started living in depravity, materialism, and idol worship again. Just as in the times of Nehemiah, our walls of faith in God were falling down and our gate being burnt! Was God unwilling to give up on our people? Was He planning to rebuild our broken walls of faith by raising up Handong Global University at the dawn of the twenty-first century? Just as He chose Nehemiah, who had no experience in construction or architecture to rebuild the broken walls of Jerusalem, was God choosing the scientist Young-Gil Kim to lead a university to be founded on Christian faith?

Did that mean that Handong, like Nehemiah, would face relentless opposition from people such as Sanballat, Tobiah, the Arabs, the Ammonites, and the men of Ashdod? (Looking back, that day's message was indeed God's word to us. After becoming the president of Handong, Young-Gil meditated on Nehemiah whenever he faced difficulties at school. The life of Nehemiah became his guide of faith, where he found God's truth and direction for his steps.) *"Surely the Sovereign Lord does nothing without revealing his plan to his servants the prophets" (Amos 3:7).*

CHAPTER 2:

From an Atheist to a Christian Scientist

A Good Heart is better Than a Smart Head

"A Good Heart is better than a Smart Head" had been my husband's family motto. His family had decided not to conform to the ways of the world. Through all their lives, his family members had been taught that it was better to be a good and generous person, even if one remained naïve, rather than being capable and smart with a poor character. His family was warm in spirit, encouraging one another even through their mistakes. Having grown up in a family of gentleness and optimism, my husband was always generous and positive.

His hometown was one of the most isolated rural areas in southeastern part of Korea, which is now under water after the construction of a dam. One of his ancestors was a prominent Confucian scholar, who was renowned for giving up his life of bureaucrat for a life of academia and devoting himself in teaching students.

My father-in-law received strict Confucian teaching from his father since the age of 12, and he was highly respected as an educated and cultured man in his typical Korean Confucian town called Andong. Andong was the city where the Queen Elizabeth II of United Kingdom visited not long ago. My husband's ancestor 34 generations back was the fourth son of the last king of the Shilla Dynasty. My father-in-law studied the Chinese classics, but he founded an elementary school for the town's children and spent his whole life as the principal of the school. He planted roses of Sharon (Korea's national flower) all along the school fences, and his school became known as the only place in Korea with the roses of Sharon at the time of Korea's liberation from Japan in 1945.

When my husband was growing up, the town was only accessible by foot within 15 miles radius from it. There were no roads, even for bicycles. He was in fourth grade in elementary school when he first saw trains, automobiles, and paved roads. He saw an airplane before ever seeing a car and dreamt that he would one day become a scientist who builds fabulous airplanes.

As the fifth of eight children, he had three older brothers, an older sister and three younger sisters. During my first "interview" with his family, his mother said, "Young-Gil has a character of a saint. I used to say that whoever married him would be a very lucky girl. But he only knows academia, so he won't do anything other than study."

You will be a Blessing

My parents used to say, "Be stingy to yourself, but be generous to your neighbors" and "A barrel of rice for a poor neighbor is money well spent, but consider precious even a single grain of rice."

My mother lived a life of virtue in a family of high repute, and her teachings to my brother and me were firm but living. My mother's hometown in the southern region was historically Confucian, and my mother was extremely strict about how a woman should carry herself, including how to stand and sit in front of elders. My mother's thriftiness did not allow leaving even a single grain of rice in my bowl. In my mother's hands, small broken things came to life again.

My father was a retired public officer who served the government his entire life as it went through three changes of administrations. He was so effective in his work that every city in which he served wanted to raise a monument in his honor. He completed his service with integrity.

My parents were extremely conservative, but they decided to send me to study in Seoul because Ewha Womans University was a prestigious Christian school and an all-women school. After completing B.A. and M.A. degree in special education, I planned to continue my study in the United States.

When I became 27 years old, my parents began to seriously worry about my getting married. I was the only daughter with one older brother. My parents did not want to discourage me from pursuing further advanced studies, but their one condition was that I marry before going abroad to study.

In 1969, I was working as a researcher at the Behavioral Science Research Center of Korea University. One day, Professor Jong-Gil Kim came to visit me in my office. He was an English literature professor at Korea University. He was known for his stylish lectures on English poems, even though he retained highly conservative upper-class traits from his Confucian hometown in Korea. He smiled at me and handed me a photograph saying,

"This is my second cousin, Young-Gil Kim, who graduated from Seoul National University with a B.S. degree in Metallurgy. He is now studying in the United States for Ph.D. in Materials Science and Engineering at Rensselaer Polytechnic Institute (RPI), Troy, New York."

I did not have the courage to look directly at the photograph, so I looked downward. Professor Kim continued,

"His elder brother, Dr. Ho-Gil Kim (then a physics professor at the University of Maryland) has been invited to participate in the Nuclear Scientific Conference in the Soviet Union in 1969. He will become the first Korean national to visit the Soviet Union. Before heading for the Soviet Union, he will be in Seoul briefly for his travel permit."

While he was in Korea, he came to see me at the school at the request of Young-Gil's parents. It was an awkward meeting for me with Young-Gil's elder brother and his relative, the English literature professor. They introduced and explained about Young-Gil again as a possible future husband of mine. They gave me several pictures, but I was too shy to look at them. So, I had a "showing myself," a kind of Korean-style bridal candidate interview without Young-Gil's presence and without being able to ask a single question about Young-Gil.

Letters from a Stranger in America

Sometime after Dr. Ho-Gil Kim returned to the United States, I received the first letter with the name 'Young-Gil Kim' written on the envelope. I opened the letter with some excitement in my heart. It was evident that he had spent much effort composing and carefully writing the letter.

Dear Young-Ae,

It is hard to think of what to write as this is the first letter of this kind. Let me first introduce myself. I was born in a traditional Confucian family in a rural town of Andong, Korea. Our family is large, and I am the youngest son among four sons and daughters. I finished my elementary and middle school in Andong, and then went to Seoul for study. After finishing undergraduate with a B.S. in Metallurgy from Seoul National University in 1964, I came over to the United States for my graduate study, and received M.S. in Metallurgy in 1969 from University of Missouri-Rolla. I am now working for Ph. D in Materials Science and Engineering at Rensselaer Polytechnic Institute, in Troy, New York. My doctorate thesis is on the development of advanced high-temperature alloys for aerospace applications. I live in a male students' dormitory of "Pardee" at room 21, and eat at student cafeteria. My sincere hope for the future is to be a scientist at NASA. I am trying my best to achieve this goal.
From Young-Gil

I was very impressed with his dream to become a scientist at NASA in the United States, although he was born and grew in a rural mountainous area in Korea. A few days later, the second letter arrived.

Dear Young-Ae,

How have you been? Have you received the letter that I sent you last time? I am anxiously waiting to receive your reply everyday. I would like to receive your latest picture. My research for Ph.D. thesis is going well, and my thesis advisor, Prof. Norman S. Stoloff, who is world-famous in high temperature alloys, is very impressed with the new results of my experiments.
From Young-Gil

Sometime later, the third letter arrived. My parents, who had known about Young-Gil's family through Korean Confucian family relationship, were enthusiastic about my writing a response to his letters. My parents felt that Young-Gil was a promising candidate for the son-in-law. I finally wrote my first letter back with care and caution.

Dear Young-Gil,

Thank you for your three letters. First of all, I would like to let you know that I am a Christian. I have attended a Presbyterian Church with my mother from my childhood. Have you ever been interested in Christianity? I always thought that I would marry someone who shares my Christian faith. I would like to know your thought and reflection on Christian faith.

From Young-Ae

After I sent my first letter, I did not receive another letter from him for a while. When I did not hear from him for almost a month, I felt regretful. Perhaps, I was too demanding and too strong about my faith in my statement. Perhaps I should have brought up the subject after we became a little more acquainted with each other. About a month later, I finally received his reply.

Dear Young-Ae,

I thought for a long time after receiving your letter. I have never thought about becoming a Christian and have never been to a church. Since I am a natural scientist, I do not believe in the existence of supernatural God. I only accept the existence of the visible material world proven by five senses and scientific experiments. But sometimes, I ask myself where the universe and I came from. After I received your letter, my deeper question became "Is there an invisible world and is there God?" With your letter, I decided to study and find out whether an almighty "Creator God" truly exists.

From Young-Gil

At least he did not seem resistant to Christianity, I thought. From that day on, we exchanged letters more frequently. His letters were simple and clear, befitting a scientist, but I could read his heart in his words and between the lines. His sincerity was manifested in every word, and his letters arrived every two to three days, sometimes two letters a day. I was moved by his dedication, which was so evident in each carefully crafted word and in each envelope decorated with different stamps. (Looking back, it is a wonder that he wrote so frequently, given how much he dislikes writing letters and how busy he must have been as he prepared for his doctoral thesis.) In appreciation of his dedication, I used to run to the Seoul Central Post Office early in the morning to buy newly issued stamps.

Dear Young-Ae,

I'm not very good at expressing my thoughts on paper, and furthermore, I'm not sure how to express my heart. These days, I feel that my heart is only filled with thoughts about you. The picture that you sent me is now sitting on my desk. I've given much thought as I read your stories. I want to marry you with all my heart. We have never talked with each other in person, but as I listened to my brother's stories and see your picture, I've become more and more convinced that you are the other half of my life. I'd very much like to know what your thoughts are about me. My dream is much more sweet and my expectations greater, perhaps, because we have never met – and I long to see you even more. I hope that all the dreams of my heart will come true. Things will be difficult until I'm finished with my studies, but I'd like to share a beautiful future with you as we understand and help each other. I wait for your reply.
From Young-Gil

My Blind Marriage

In the fall of 1969, I received a proposal from a man whom I have never met before. And I accepted his proposal! Many letters arrived from him, as well as many international phone calls. In those days, we had to make a reservation to the phone company in order to make an international call and wait for a long time to be connected. Sometimes my mother and my aunt would amuse themselves as they eavesdropped on our conversations.

On the other hand, my friends were incredulous. "Who in this day and age gets married based only on a photograph! This is a huge gamble! Are you out of your mind?"

Despite their reproving advice, my heart was at peace.

The winter passed, and the new year came. On June 8, 1970, the night before his arrival from the United States, I could not fall asleep. Thoughts about the famous Korean novelist Bi-Suk Chung's *"Wildflowers"* passed through my head. It was about a bride who had her wedding dress and veil prepared only to run away the day before the wedding. I wondered, 'What if I'm so disappointed at my fiancé tomorrow that I want to run away, when a banquet room has already been reserved and the invitation cards sent out?'

On the day that I was to meet my fiancé in person for the first time, I went to the airport with my mother. She seemed quite nervous as she prepared to meet the son-in-law whom she had only seen in a photograph. She knew everything about his family, nevertheless she was extremely curious to see what kind of a person her only son-in-law would turn out to be.

"Mother, there he comes. It's him!" I said.

"I guess he's your other half – you recognized him right away!" she said.

I knew him as soon as I saw him. Wearing a winter suit in early summer, with black horn-rimmed glasses and unkempt long hair, it was unmistakably him. He was definitely not a man of style. Having to finish his doctoral examinations before flying to Korea six days before his wedding, he had no time for a haircut. In the previous winter, I had sent him a winter suit as an engagement gift, and he wore that suit on his flight home to make it easier for us to recognize him. He was a very practical and straightforward man.

My mother, who had a traditional view of a good husband as an aristocratic looking man with light skin and some weight on his body, seemed quite disappointed. Despite more than four years of life in the United States, there was nothing about him that seemed refined.

"Mother, do you like him?" I asked cautiously.

"I'm satisfied if you are," he answered.

I was concerned about her lukewarm response. He seemed unsophisticated, but I had already chosen him in my heart. My mother, before leaving for Daegu city ahead of me to prepare for the wedding ceremony, ordered, "Young-Ae, we should choose a navy blue suit for him for the ceremony. Black makes him look even skinnier. And he should have a haircut before anything else."

We sat across from each other for the first time at a café in downtown Seoul. Things had been much more natural when we were communicating with letters. I had been so happy when he called from the United States. But now that we were actually sitting by ourselves face to face, we could only look at each other without being able to say a word.

He took something out of his pocket. I looked at him across the table, hoping that this awkward scene would somehow turn around. He showed me four American coins – a penny, a dime, a nickel, and a quarter.

"This is made with copper, and this one is made of nickel alloy," he talked as if this explanation were of utmost importance.

'A lecture on American coins on our first date – how befitting for a metallurgical engineer,' I thought.

It turned out to be a completely insipid first date.

The next evening, my brother invited him for dinner. After dinner, my brother got up and disappeared. A few minutes later, I could hear him through the walls talking to my mother on the phone.

"Mother, he seems much better than yesterday. Don't worry. If he eats well for the next few days or so, he'll gain some weight and look better."

'Doesn't he know that Young-Gil could hear everything too? How could he speak so loudly?' I thought.

My brother was right, though. Having gotten a fresh haircut, he did look much better than the day before.

When he saw my mother at the Daegu train station the next day, he scratched his head and said with a smile on his face, "Do I look okay today?"

My mother was surprised by such an unexpected question, but as if pleased with his healthier look and his cheerful greeting, she shot a glance at me with a teasing smile.

"You told on me, didn't you? Siding with your husband-to-be already...."

On June 15, 1970, one year after the 'showing myself' to his brother and cousin, and exchanging our hearts only through letters and phone calls, we were married.

He Told Me about Gospel's Truth

In order to keep his promise to me, Young-Gil attended church every Sunday after we were married. Having started reading the Bible, he constantly asked me questions.

"It could've said that Joseph and Mary married and gave birth to Jesus, but why on earth would it say that he was conceived by the Holy Spirit? Who can believe such nonsense and unscientific reasoning? And how can water turn into wine instantly? Even if there were a fusion reaction, this is taking things too far. If I can acknowledge such miracles, what is the point of my research? On top of this, it says that Jesus fed 5,000 people with two fish and five loaves of bread. Rather than a material alteration, this is an expansion in mass and volume – an even greater miracle than water being turned into wine! This violates a fundamental law of science, 'the law of the conservation of mass.' The Bible is full of such illogical inconsistencies, and it is too difficult for a person like me to believe in it."

I had accompanied my mother to church ever since I was a child, and had always been diligent at church work. But I did not have the biblical knowledge to answer all of my husband's questions, and so whenever I lacked an answer, I could only threaten him saying,

"God would not be very pleased if you argue with him about all these scientific laws. You have to just believe in the Bible, no questions asked!"

Young-Gil replied, "Well, I have seen the Bible containing things that we should accept, in addition to things that I cannot acknowledge. Christianity's morality seems a level higher than all other religions. In Confucian teachings, I've never heard that one should love even his enemy. So, I guess it's better to educate our children with Christianity. I will keep going to church although I can't believe in the Bible."

When Young-Gil was working at NASA Lewis Research Center in Cleveland, Ohio in 1974, a few friends at our Cleveland Korean Church started praying for his faith. There were even friends who prayed with fasting for him. At last, Young-Gil started to read earnestly many apologetics and inspiring Christian books. In the week of the Easter in 1974, he was immersed in reading several books, even forgetting his dinner.

"Dinner is ready," I said.

"Dinner isn't important right now!" he replied.

I had never seen him like that. I understood that something was moving in his spirit. After many hours, he asked me to come and sit next to him. He told me why he should accept and believe the existence of the God Creator as a scientist.

"I cannot doubt the existence of the Creator God based on the scientific reasoning of cause and effect. In the physical world, there are laws, orders, genetic information, and harmony. Based on the scientific reasoning of cause and effect, laws are established by lawmakers, and orders are produced by intelligence. But nothing can exist without the cause, and the First cause here is the Creator God. It is illogical to believe that something could begin to exist without an intelligent cause. A computer implies a computer maker. This universe is the work of God and a product of His design. Now, I came to realize a total comprehensive worldview that covers all aspects of the world. One is the visible material world, and the other is the invisible spiritual world. So far, I accepted and believed only in the existence of the visible material world. But, the invisible does not mean the nonexistence. The invisible is invisible because it is outside the scientific realm. God is the invisible Spirit, and therefore we cannot see Him with our naked eyes. God created both visible and invisible worlds. There are four levels in the visible natural world: The lowest is the atomic world, then, the plant, the animal, and the highest of these is the human world. The fifth and the highest level of them all is the invisible supernatural world. God ordained the laws for each world and level. For example, in the world of atoms, physics law governs the rotation of electrons around protons. God created biological laws for living things, such as growth and multiplication. When God created human beings, He gave moral and spiritual laws. The laws of the higher world contain and override the laws of the lower world. In geometry, lines consist of numerous spots, planes consist of many lines, and a solid cube comprises numerous planes.

As I began to comprehend that there were gradations in creation, I came to understand that a lower level of life can never fathom a higher one. When animals observe the human world- people driving a car, operating a computer, flying an airplane- they cannot comprehend what is going on. These instruments are miracle to animals, but not to a modern man. A miracle to an animal cannot be a miracle to a human being. Just as a dog or donkey cannot understand how to fly an airplane or operate a computer, can we not see that God's mighty acts are far richer and greater than we can ever comprehend? Turning water into wine is a miracle to human beings, but is natural in the supernatural world when God intervenes.

I will tell you more about miracles. We call something a 'miracle' when it contradicts our common sense or cannot be understood by our human knowledge of the world. Physics laws assume that no other natural or supernatural factors are interfering with the operation that the scientific laws govern. If I raise a stone with my hand, the law of gravitation acting on the stone is not violated or negated, but it is overcome by a greater force of my muscle. The stone cannot raise itself by its own force. However, if the stone were raised by a force invisible to me, I may consider an incident as a miracle because I cannot see the force. Whether or not I can see the force does not affect the operation itself. Miracles lie outside the realm of natural science that can be experimented based on our five senses. The acceptance of miracles requires a 'quantum jump or leap' from the limits of the visible material world into the invisible spiritual realm. There is no conflict between science and miracle. They are not really contradictory to each other, but they are actually compatible. The miracles Jesus performed are not the subjects of scientific investigation or interpretation, but are powerful signs that Jesus Christ Himself is the Creator of the universe!! Now, I have no problem in believing all the miracles Jesus performed when I believe that Jesus is the Creator. God created the good universe, but we are now fallen creatures in the fallen world due to our sins. Because of God's great love for His creation, He desires to restore the broken relationship. There is no single person in the world and in the entire human history who is without sin, and thus, eligible to pay the penalty for the human sin. So, God devised a way in which He Himself could pay the penalty for our sins. Jesus Christ came to earth to die on the cross to pay a ransom for my sins, a sinner, and He saved me!"

As I listened to him, I could not understand well all the scientific explanations, but I was so happy to listen to his scientific reasoning of faith as a scientist. For me, all the jig-saw puzzle pieces of mysterious Bible knowledge from my early childhood suddenly came together. I had been oblivious to the truth despite my many years of church life, an empty-minded church member who knew only of religious rituals. When my spiritual eyes were finally opened from blindness, tears of thanksgiving flowed as I realized the infinite love of God for us. I said to Young-Gil, "Jesus Christ died on the cross for our sins on our behalf, and resurrected from the dead!"

In the Easter week of 1974, we both received Jesus Christ as our Lord and Savior, and were born again by the Holy Spirit, becoming a new creation in Christ.

"To all who received him, to those who believed in his name, he gave the right to become children of God" (John 1:12).

The Bible verse *"So the last will be first, and the first will be last" (Matthew 20:16)* had been written for the two of us. Young-Gil and I knelt down and prayed together as a new member of God's family.

"Dear Heavenly Father God! Thank you for saving us from our sins and giving us eternal life. Please lead us and use us as your instrument to proclaim the Good News. Empower us with your Holy Spirit to become a witness of your Kingdom and your glory." On that day, Young-Gil was born again as "Nehemiah" Young-Gil Kim.

Instead of Alcohol, Water of Life

My husband liked to drink very much. His friends in college remembered him as a great drinker. In the basement of my in-laws' house, there was always aromatic rice wine stored in preparation for the monthly ancestral ceremonies. However, he used to pride himself on having been taught the proper etiquette of drinking.

During his graduate study for Ph.D. at RPI in Troy, New York, he always bought a case of Johnny Walker on his way back from visiting his elder brother in Washington D.C., since alcohol was cheaper there than in the New York State. One day, after driving on the freeway for a while from Maryland to New York, he stopped his car, opened the trunk and said, "Hey bottles, let's make it home safely without getting broken."

We had all kinds of recipe books and equipment for making cocktails. We even had a small bar in the corner of our living room where bottles were displayed. During meals, he sometimes made sweet, aromatic cocktails for me. But after accepting Christ, I became concerned about all those bottles of alcohol and his drinking habit.

When I prayed, "Lord, please help him stop drinking," he objected.

"I didn't say 'Amen.' Why do you pray to God about my drinking? I enjoy drinking, but I don't get drunk or make mistakes. Where in the Bible does it say not to drink? Even Paul gave wine to Timothy. Don't tell God about that again."

So I began to pray for him in secret. One day, a friend at church gave me some sermon tapes titled *"Do not get drunk on wine, which leads to debauchery. Instead, be filled with the Spirit" (Ephesians 5:18)* by Pastor Kyung-Jik Han, the founder of the Youngnak Presbyterian Church in Seoul and later, a winner of Templeton Freedom Award.

"All of us Christians are in a race. Does anyone run with heavy clothes and high heels? We run with shorts and bare feet. A Christian who lives a life of faith with unbeneficial habits of the world is like a runner who runs with heavy clothes and sandbags on his legs."

This was it! That night, I surreptitiously began playing the sermon tape. Young-Gil's face became more and more serious as he listened. After thinking for a while, he suddenly got up and went to the mini bar. I immediately knew what he was about to do.

I encouraged him. "Young-Gil, throw away the opened bottles, but save the unopened ones. We can take them as gifts when we're invited for dinners."

"How can I give someone things that I think is unfit for myself?" he questioned.

He poured all those bottles down the drain, one by one. As the alcohol drained away, water of life was pouring upon us. I could not explain in words the joy we felt after throwing away all the bottles of alcohol. From that day on, he never touched alcohol again. It was not by human willpower. God had changed his habits and tastes. After he returned to Korea, his old drinking buddies were extremely disappointed by how he had changed.

"You're not the same after going to the United States and becoming a Christian. You've become a boring person because of Jesus," they remarked.

I said to Young-Gil, "You've been so blessed by believing in Jesus Christ. If you had continued drinking, your nose would be strawberry red by now."

Homecoming Wish

After working at NASA in Cleveland, Young-Gil moved to the Research & Development Center of the International Nickel Company (INCO) in Suffern, New York. He wanted the practical experience in the manufacturing company to expand his scientific career. We lived in a beautiful town of Monroe in the State of New York, where we could see the forest and a lake in one sweep, but it was also a lonely place where there was almost no Korean. Perhaps that was what triggered in my heart a desire to return to Korea. However, the biggest reason was the need to introduce Jesus Christ to our aging parents-in-law and my father.

"For it is God who works in you to will and to act according to his good purpose" (Philippians 2:13). I told Young-Gil how I felt.

"My plan is to build more research experience in the States before going back to Korea. Why don't you pray about it and ask what God's will is?" he answered.

He gave me the burden of prayer instead. I too was hesitant to give up our life of comfort and our children's education in the States. Also, it was not easy for him to give up a career that others envied. At that time, the former US President Jimmy Carter announced his plan to withdraw American troops from Korea. When rumors of a war became rampant, we briefly hesitated. But then, my mother sent me a letter.

"It is when our country is in difficult times that young people like you must return home and become a source of strength for our country."

Ultimately, Young-Gil turned in his resignation to INCO. His boss at the research center, Dr. Howard Merrick, fervently opposed his decision.

"I think you're homesick, having been away from Korea for too long. How about taking a month of vacation there, or a six-month leave of absence?"

His elder brother Dr. Ho-Gil Kim, who was a senior scientist at the Lawrence Laboratory of UC Berkeley at the time, also tried to convince us to stay in the States. But we decided not to hesitate any more, and not to compare the conditions in Korea with those in the States. In 1979, our family permanently returned to Korea, and my husband took a post of professorship at the Material Science Department of the Korea Advanced Institute of Science and Technology (KAIST), which was established to attract top-notch scientific manpower from overseas.

We felt very different on our flight back home. In 1967, Young-Gil had left to study abroad with $150 in his pockets, the maximum amount Korean government allowed for traveling overseas. Twelve years later, we recounted the blessings that God had bestowed upon us. Young-Gil had received his doctorate degree and built a research career of seven years at NASA and INCO, and we were now returning to Korea with our son Jimmy Ho-Min, who was 9 years old, and our daughter Joann Jong-Min, who was 7 years old. We were thankful that Young-Gil had been able to study on a graduate Research Assistantship under the guidance of Dr. Norman S. Stoloff and with distinguished colleagues. We were very thankful to the University, NASA and INCO among others.

First and foremost, though, we gave our thanks to God. We were returning to our homeland with a new perspective on life, a new value system, and most importantly, a new purpose for our lives.

"Therefore, if anyone is in Christ, he is a new creation; the old has gone, the new has come!" (II Corinthians 5:17).

Meeting with Christian Scientists

When Young-Gil was working as a Professor at the Korea Advance Institute of Science & Technology (KAIST) in 1980, new Christian relationships were waiting for him at the Science Research

Community in Seoul, where the various Government research institutes were located. Many scientists who had been recruited from abroad had returned to Korea as Christians. Over 50% of the people in the Research Community were believers, the highest proportion of Christians in Korea for any groups at that time. These Christian relationships paved the way for the birth of the Korea Association for Creation Research (KACR) later.

In August 1980, the International Conference entitled, "The Origin of Life: Evolution or Creation?" was held in Seoul, during the 1980 World Evangelical Congress. The Conference was organized by the Korea Campus Crusade for Christ (KCCC). The Keynote speakers from the States were Dr. Henry M. Morris, the founder of Institute for Creation Research (ICR), Dr. Duane Gish, Vice President, of the ICR, Professor Walter Bradley of Texas A&M University, and Dr. Charles B. Thaxton.

The Conference organizer had been looking for a domestic speaker majoring in life science. They contacted a number of promising speakers, but they all declined the invitation, explaining that it would be awkward for them to deliver lectures denying the theory of evolution as life scientists. Y. Shim, who was then a master's student in chemistry at Korea University and an administrator of KCCC came to see Young-Gil. But, he also turned down his request, excusing that he did not have enough professional knowledge as his major field was not life science. Mr. Shim did not take "no" for an answer. Young-Gil, as a person who liked the phrase "ignorance breeds courage," said himself, "If no one is willing to step up for the job, then I will consider it God's command and will obey."

Faced with a huge task suddenly, he diligently read through an armful of books on the origin of life published by the Institute for Creation Research (ICR) in San Diego, California, and other creationism groups. The two-day conference was held on August 13 and 14, 1980, to debate on the origin of life. Over the two-day period, more than 4,000 people attended the conference. He prepared his talk on "Scientific Views of the Origin of Life," and presented it at the conference. He was very tense because it was the first time in his life that he presented a paper to the large audience in a creation science seminar. But, the seminar had attracted considerable attention because they had never heard the contradictions of evolutionism and the scientific evidences of creationism before. After the conference, Young-Gil have been invited by numerous churches, Christian schools, universities, and organizations for his presentation of creation science seminars since 1981. Faith in creation is the very foundation of Biblical world view and Christian education. That is why Young-Gil decided to include creation science as a core course for all students at Handong Global University from the beginning in 1995. Young-Gil was elected as the founding president of Korea Association for Creation Research(KACR) in 1981, and served until 1994.

Back to Alma Mater

Until I got married in 1970, my dream was to teach at my alma mater, Ewha Womans University, which was founded in 1886 by Mrs. Mary F. Scranton, an American Methodist missionary, as the country's first woman-only Christian university. But after accepting Jesus Christ as my Lord and Savior, my priority changed. Also, since I had to raise the children, my advanced graduate study slowed-down.

One day when our children were in elementary school and kindergarten, Young-Gil took me to the State University of New York (SUNY) at New Paltz, located about an hour-drive away from our home. With Young-Gil's support, I registered to continue my studies for a doctorate's degree in Special Education, but I had to return to Korea without finishing the degree.

About a year after my return, one of my professors at Ewha Woman University asked me to lecture there starting from the spring semester. I was overjoyed, but I was soon worried whether I could teach well. I was to teach theories and give advices in creating teaching material for handicapped children, but that was not my field of expertise. Furthermore, unlike the United States where there were many text books available on this subject, the state of Korean special education at that time was dismal to the point of a dire absence of teaching material. I was unsure whether I should accept the offer. So I prayed to God for help.

"Oh Lord, if you're calling me to teach at Ewha and be a tool to spread the Gospel, then give me the necessary books."

The deadline to respond to Ewha's offer was approaching, but I did not yet have the books of the related subjects. Just the day before the deadline, however, God faithfully answered my prayer with precision in an unexpected way: A friend of mine, who learned my situation, brought an armful of material and books on visual and auditory senses from a U.S. military base book store in Seoul!

I spent the whole winter preparing for my lectures with excitement because I could feel God's presence with me. But when the first day of school arrived, I became fearful. Wanting further confirmation from God, I prayed,

"Lord, if you let me meet two of your people tomorrow at school, then I will take it as a sign that you are pleased with this work."

The next day as I left home with a nervous heart, Young-Gil asked, "Oh good! Can you deliver my article to the Ewha newspaper office for me?"

When I arrived at school, I called the newspaper office from the department's office. A graduate student, who had overheard my phone conversation, asked, "Is your husband Dr. Young-Gil Kim?"

"Yes," I answered.

"Hallelujah! My friend and I have been praying for a long time that God would send a Christian professor to our department. God has answered our prayers!" she exclaimed.

How could there be a clearer confirmation from God than this? I thanked God.

"Lord, I will do my best to teach my students well, and I will share the Gospel in my final lecture."

For the next 14 years, God protected my health and my circumstances so that I never missed a lecture or arrived late to class. I lacked in so many areas, but the one thing that I could teach my students with confidence was "responsibility and faithfulness." I believed that taking responsibility for one's work and living with sincerity and dedication were far more important than ability. Sometimes when I entered the classroom early, some students would complain, "Professor, it's not time yet!"

"I'm sorry, there indeed is another minute to go. But if I'm late by one minute, then it will be like one person wasting 70 minutes since there are 70 of you."

The semester passed and the final lecture time came. I began to speak as if the entire semester had existed for this one last hour. Even the students who had been busy preparing for finals lifted their heads and began to listen.

"People cannot be transformed because of knowledge gained in one semester. The ones who fight in wars are people, not weapons. Before any great teaching material or knowledge, the most important thing is the teacher. You have to teach the disabled children with faithfulness, always being conscious that God's eyes are on you. Even when the teacher does not do a good job, no one will blame the teacher but instead the child's handicap. But God knows everything.

Special education is a field with the promise of God's blessings. Even when you get discouraged while teaching handicapped children, remember that you are studying a field with promises for this life and the next. Jesus said in the Bible, ***"But when you give a banquet, invite the poor, the crippled, the lame, the blind, and you will be blessed. Although they cannot repay you, you will be repaid at the resurrection of the righteous" (Luke14:13-14).*** Man's love has limits. Man's love, love based on reason, can change depending on circumstances. Only those who have received true love can love someone else. God's love never changes.

"God so loved us that He sent us His only son to die on the cross for us. The Bible says that whoever believes in this truth will have eternal life. Once you discover what God's love for you is like, your lives will change beyond your wildest imaginations. Don't be shy toward God, but instead embrace His love like little children."

Then I read them a poem that I loved.

Dear Friend,

How are you? I just had to send you a note to tell you how much I care about you.

I saw you yesterday as you were talking with your friends. I waited all day hoping you would want to talk to me, too. I gave you a sunset to close your day and a cool breeze to rest you — and I waited. You never came. It hurt me, but I will love you because I am your friend.

I saw you sleeping last night and longed to touch your brow, so I spilled moonlight upon your face. Again I waited, wanting to rush down so we could talk. I have so many gifts for you! You awoke late and rushed off to work. My tears were the rain.

Oh, if you only knew how much I want to walk and talk with you. We could spend an eternity together in heaven. I know how hard it is on the earth, I really know! And I want to help you. I want you to meet my father. He wants to help you too. My father is that way, you know.

Just call me, ask me, talk with me. Oh, please don't forget me. I have so much to share with you.

All right, I won't bother you any further. You are free to choose me or not, it's your decision. However, I will wait you, because I love you.
Your Friend,
Jesus
(Author Unknown)

One student who had been listening to me started to cry. All of a sudden, I too choked up. I turned my face away, trying not to look at the student, and I finished that day's last lecture. A few days later, I received a letter at home.

"As I listened to your words that day, my spirit awoke from the sleep."

It was from the student who had cried in class. After graduation, she became a special education teacher and has sent me many letters since then, saying, "I will try to share with my students the joy I felt when you introduced me to Jesus."

Is the Dragon-king Greater than Jesus?

In 1979, soon after returning to Korea, Young-Gil earnestly talked with his mother to share the Gospel.

"Mother! The Bible says that all humans are sinners. Have you ever thought that you were a sinner?"

"Sure, I'm a sinner too. There's nothing so evil as humans! We eat everything off the fields, we eat out of the ocean, and we catch birds in the air. And yet, the words out of people's mouths are evil.

When I walk outside at night, it's more frightening to run into a man than an animal! That tells me that people are sinners! I too have a lot of sins. Yes, many sins!"

His mother accepted Jesus Christ that night.

"For it is with your heart that you believe and are justified, and it is with your mouth that you confess and are saved" (Romans 10:10).

But wanting to make sure that she did the right thing, she secretly asked her third son, Ho-Gil.

"Ho-Gil! In your opinion, who is greater, the dragon-king or Jesus?"

I strained to listen to the conversation from the other room. I was curious as to how he would respond. She seemed to be intently waiting for his answer. Smiling at his mother's childlike question, he replied, "Mother! Think of Jesus as the bigger house, and the dragon-king as the smaller house. If you're going to believe in something, you might as well believe in the bigger house."

Relieved to hear her son's humorous answer, she said, "You think so too? Thanks!"

Sometime later, she came to Seoul for her baptism, and she bowed down deep when she met the pastor. "Pastor, thank you very much!"

She was advanced in years, and though she could not attend church regularly, she read the Bible and prayed every day. One of our nieces visited her over winter break, and she reported back to me, "Aunt Young-Ae! Grandmother still went down to the river this full moon to prepare an offering for the dragon-king."

When Young-Gil's mother came to Seoul, I asked her, "Mother! You were baptized because you professed Jesus as your Lord. Don't you think you shouldn't be serving the dragon-king anymore?"

She seemed dejected at my knowing about this and replied, "Who told you that? My dear, even humans are hurt when you cut off the relation all of a sudden. I went down to the river to tell him that I won't be coming back anymore. That was my last."

Since then, every morning, she recited the Lord's Prayer and the Apostle's Creed. When she lost her place once in a while, she would say, "Oh God, I'm sorry! I forgot where I was, so I'll start over." She prayed as if singing an old, traditional Korean folk song.

One day, she said, "Young-Gil! When I read the Bible, I found that you resembled Joseph! He spent a long time overseas and then, he became a blessing to his country and his family. You too will be like him!"

We were overjoyed to see her reading and understanding the Bible. *"Believe in the Lord Jesus, and you will be saved – you and your household" (Acts 16:31).*

Keep it a Secret!

In October 1986, when my father-in-law returned from the closing ceremony of the Asian Olympic Games in Seoul, his face looked downcast. A few days later, he told us what had been bothering him. On his cab ride to the stadium in Seoul, the driver started talking to him.

"You came all the way from the countryside to see the ceremony! You look very happy."

"Yes, everybody tells me that I am a lucky man!"

"But do you believe in Jesus Christ?"

"I don't, but my son, my daughter-in-law and my grandchildren all attend church."

"You're about to see the closing ceremony, but you can't enter the place without a ticket. Likewise, if you don't have your own ticket to heaven, then it's no good since you cannot enter it. You seem to be full in years, so how about preparing the ticket to heaven by believing in Jesus?"

We could not let this opportunity pass. With courage, we explained to him who Jesus was. It was not easy to explain that "you too are a sinner" to such a well-respected man. After listening to us for some time, he said, "My grandson Ho-Min likes to talk to me when I come over to your house, and when I listen carefully to what he says, he talks about Jesus. In your house, even the kids are all wrapped up in Jesus!"

Young-Gil gave his father "The Four Spiritual Laws" written in Chinese characters. That day, my father-in-law prayed and accepted Jesus Christ.

"God! I hadn't realized that living my life without knowing you was a sin. From now on, I receive Jesus Christ as my Lord and

Savior. I pray that you will protect me until I go to heaven." Ho-Min, who was in junior high school at the time, secretly recorded his grandfather's prayer.

"Grandfather, I have your prayer recorded on a tape, so from now on, you have to tell everyone that you believe in Jesus. We have proof here."

"Hey! You guys are worse than a spy sting operation! Okay, I have a ticket to heaven now just like you, so don't worry about me anymore. But don't tell anyone else about it. Just keep it a secret! What would people think if they find out that I believe in Jesus at my age?"

After a few months, he came to Seoul to be baptized at the Onnuri Presbyterian Church. He said to Pastor Ha, "I came because I was told that each person has to get his own ticket to heaven."

It was his first visit to church in his life. On a Friday afternoon, in an empty sanctuary, several pastors surrounded my father-in-law on the stage and performed the baptism ceremony. Looking at him on his knees, all of us cried with tears of joy. My sister-in-law, who had only recently started going to church, said, "My father getting baptized is truly an earth-shattering event!"

"Salvation is found in no one else, for there is no other name under heaven given to men by which we must be saved" (Acts 4:12).

How Can I Believe if He is Dead?

My mother grew up in a family that strictly followed the teaching of Confucianism. When she was a girl, she met a Christian for the first time in her life. This Christian was a traveling saleswoman, who sold sundry items such as silk, face powder, and sewing material. She had been notorious for mistreating her husband's children from a previous marriage. However, she changed after becoming a Christian, and now the whole town was full of praise for how good she was to her children. When she visited a home, she was more interested in talking about Jesus than in selling her goods. Sometimes, she would sing a hymn with a look of bliss on her face: "Those who love the Lord will soar like an eagle." My mother was curious about who this Jesus was, and she would eagerly listen to the saleswoman's stories.

And so the seed of salvation was planted in my mother early. After getting married, she became a Christian with the help of a relative and began her walk of faith. My mother was devoted to my father and served him to be the happy head of the household, but she was unable to lead him to Christ. My husband and I spent many anxious years before we were able to witness God to him.

In 1977, when my father traveled to the United States on a business trip and visited us in our home for the first time, we desperately tried to tell him about the Gospel. He seemed a bit disappointed that his daughter would only talk about Jesus when he was seeing her for the first time in nearly 10 years.

After returning to Korea, I tried to evangelize him whenever I had a chance. Then one day, when I told him about Jesus dying on the cross, he fell on the floor and said, "Oh no! That's why I said I couldn't believe in him. How can I believe if he's dead?"

There was one hurdle after another, but I did not give up – I climbed over one hurdle at a time with him. In order to please him, Young-Gil had to play many games of Chinese chess with him. Sitting next to them, I would beg him again and again, "Father, just one more game and we're going to church tonight, yes?"

One game would lead to another, sometimes two or three more. But this was why we had returned to Korea! Finally, my father was led to church. Fortunately, there was a revival meeting that evening. Both my father and his brother, who had come along, were wide-eyed at all the people who were singing with their arms raised. When they started singing, "Father, I Stretch my Hands to Thee," my father smiled and whispered to me, "I know this melody well, but do you know that your mother can't sing? After all those years at church, all her hymns have the same melody."

Singing along with the congregation with arms raised, my father looked like a captive who had surrendered to God. I was overjoyed, half laughing and half crying. After retirement, my father and my mother helped with a start-up church. My father named the church as "Myung-hyun" meaning "bright and upright church that spreads the Word of God," and he proactively helped with church work.

Sometime later, my father was suddenly hospitalized. To our utter surprise, it was a stomach cancer. Whenever there was an opportunity, I talked to him once again with all my heart to confirm his faith. From his hospital bed, he asked many questions about all the things of which he had been unsure. Eventually he prayed a confession from his heart that he was a sinner before God and that Jesus Christ had died for all his sins. It was exactly three years since our return to Korea.

"Father, now you must be baptized."

"I should be baptized in a church," he said, but when his condition worsened day by day, I decided that he needed to be baptized right away. The next day, without prior notice, the senior pastor of Myung-hyun Church visited us at the hospital in Seoul. He had come prepared to baptize my father.

"Pastor, how did you know to come prepared?" I asked.

"The Holy Spirit told me," he answered.

Three days after his baptism, my father went to be in God's arms with great peace. He was 64. Life truly belongs to God; at the very end of his life, my father accepted Jesus Christ as his Lord and Savior, and was even used by God in starting a church.

And so Young-Gil and I delivered the Word of God in our workplaces and within our family. But even then, we could not imagine how God's plans for our future would unfold.

PART II: ADVENTURE

CHAPTER 3:

Stumbling Blocks

A Family Tragedy

In the first week of April 1994, Young-Gil started to work for the preparation of a new educational venture of Handong Global University, and stayed with his elder brother Ho-Gil at the official residence of the President of Pohang University of Science and Technology (POSTECH). Young-Gil learned experience and knowledge about university president's roles from his brother. He was very happy that he could stay with his elder brother in Pohang city. In March 1994, a major Korean daily new paper wrote an article titled, "Two Brothers as University Presidents in the Same City" and reported that two brothers who had both pursued careers in science were now both presidents of universities in Pohang city.

On April 30, 1994, when Young-Gil had just arrived in Seoul from Pohang, the phone rang. It was an out of breath voice.

"This is POSTECH. The president has been in a tragic accident. He fell while playing a soft-baseball tournament between POSTECH and POSCO Research Institute. He hit his head against a corner of a breast wall. Unfortunately…."

"What? What did you say?"

"Doctors didn't have time to do anything."

Young-Gil fell to the floor. How could this happen when he had just seen his brother that morning? How could there be such an unfortunate death? His parents were still alive and were over 80 years old. How could there be such terrible news? Young-Gil wailed as if a part of his body had been torn off.

His brother had been a man of exceptional intelligence. He received his Ph.D. in nuclear physics from University of Birmingham in the United Kingdom. Afterwards, he was with the Lawrence Radiation Laboratory at UC Berkley, and he was a professor of Physics at University of Maryland prior to returning to Korea. From childhood, he was a teacher and a mentor to Young-Gil. When his elder brother returned to Korea after 23 years in the United States, his parents could not express their joy for having their sons back in their home country. Who knew that such a tragedy would strike only 10 years later?

After the sudden loss of Young-Gil's brother, we were even more fearful of going to Pohang. The founder tried to comfort Young-Gil. "If Dr. Ho-Gil Kim had been around, he would have been of tremendous help to our school. But President Kim! God's plan is in all of this. He must not be allowing two giants in one city at the same time. I pray that you will work for the roles of both of you through Handong."

Young-Gil lamented.

A Sudden Calamity on Founder's Business

It seemed that the bigger the dream, the more obstacles we must overcome. We hoped for a smooth launch of Handong, but the first obstacle came much too soon. On June 20, 1994, while Young-Gil was in the United States to recruit professors, I was shocked to see an article in the newspaper. There was a major accident at the company that the founder directed. Since we had been steadily preparing for the school's opening, I was at a loss. Who could then imagine that this was only a part of the waves of obstacles that Handong would face in the future?

I delivered the news to Young-Gil and he went directly to the school upon his arrival to Korea. The founder tried to reassure us, but sometime later, rumors began to spread that his company would be sold and that Handong would be unable to open the following year. At the end of July 1994, an extreme heat wave continued day after day, but Young-Gil threw himself into preparing for the opening as if he had no other worries. Then, just as we feared, the founder told us that all plans for opening the school would have to be cancelled. He suggested to Young-Gil to seek help from the Korean Christian community or look for a Christian businessperson who could support the school, since Handong was to be founded on Christian principles.

What should we do? Should we act on common sense or on faith? We had received a test from God, and we fell into a deep quicksand of worries. In some ways, it seemed irrelevant for the president to agonize over what to do considering that the founder had given up the school.

Had we simply said, "There could have been a genuine Christian university, but it was not God's will," who would confront us and say, "Do not use God's name according to your own will?" How many people would mourn over the fact that such a university had almost been founded but failed? Deep inside, I was glad in some ways. But still deeper inside, a voice that I could not deny spoke out, "Can the God you believe in do His work only when your businesses go well? Has He no other resources? Have you believed in God only as a notion? You have been declaring to others that God is a God of creation who creates out of nothing, but were those declarations mere confessions of your lips?"

The test from God examined our faith, and the answer seemed all too clear. How then could we choose a different answer?

"God, you are the living and almighty God."

I offered confessions of faith when I was on my knees in prayer, but when I opened my eyes, I looked for a way to escape from all anxieties. Did faith always accompany such fearful crisis? The difficulty of making the decision to become the first Handong Global University's president paled in comparison with the one we faced now. We wanted to run away from God's eyes, but whenever our hearts were filled with such thoughts, God's voice seemed to ring out yet again.

"Show me your confession of faith with your lives. Knowing your fears and worries, I have already shown you my will several times. I have even spoken to you through those with wisdom and foresight. Do not fear, but proceed with this work. And trust me!"

Mother's Death

Young-Gil's mother passed away that year. Six months after burying her third son Ho-Gil, his mother too had left this world. She had always been a source of limitless warmth and comfort but now, she was no longer around when her youngest son was in such a difficult situation. Wearing his black mourning clothes, Young-Gil looked infinitely sad and lonely.

Was God telling us to rely on nothing else – including our family – but to trust Him only by taking away those whom we trusted and depended on? While we were still in mourning, the chief of a conglomerate who had visited us a few months before sent an urgent message wanting to see Young-Gil right away. We hurriedly left for Seoul. The school's situation did not seem to allow even a period of mourning for our mother.

The next day, Young-Gil came back from the meeting, looking utterly dejected. When he saw me, he shook his head. The collars on his coat were flying like lonely flags in the wind. My heart sank. What should we do now? The hope that we had held onto for the last three months was suddenly cut off. The head of the conglomerate told Young-Gil with great difficulty, "I don't have the confidence to pull it off no matter how much I think about it. I don't have the courage to start a new university when I'm over 80 years old. If I were just 10 years younger…."

Young-Gil let out an empty laugh and said, "What can we do? Apparently, God isn't allowing it. We just have to look for someone else."

"Then why couldn't he let us know earlier? How can he tell us now, after all the delays, that he can't do it?"

I resented that businessman in my heart. If he had not taken such a long time to decide, we would have given up on him much earlier and would not have become this much involved in Handong affairs. But was God's will present even in this situation? Thinking that God had held onto that man for this long to make sure that we did not back out, my resentment subsided. Still, even if that were so, what could we do about this stark reality? Because of the media's continuous and positive coverage, Handong's launch the next year was well publicized. Newly recruited professors from abroad were also hurriedly preparing to relocate in Korea. We could not give up now.

If You Repent

Deep in our worries, we did not even feel the summer heat. Early every morning, I ran to church and prayed. But one morning, when I awoke, my body felt as if it weighed a ton. I wanted to rest for just that one day. So, I picked up the phone to call Mrs. Lee, who came to pick me up every morning, but I hung up without calling.

"Lord, I'm so tired today. Can't I rest just this one day?"

I whined to God. He seemed to say to me, "I awoke you from your sleep, so why don't you want to pray?"

As soon as I sat down in the car, I pushed the seat back and closed my eyes. I said to Mrs. Lee, "I was going to skip today."

"Really? I also wanted to skip today because I didn't feel well. But I came because I thought you would be waiting for me," she said.

"We will be blessed today since we were both tempted not to go this morning," I remarked.

When we entered the sanctuary, I sat in my usual seat and closed my eyes without even opening the Bible. The pastor started reading the Scripture. *"Therefore, this is what the Lord says: 'If you repent, I will restore you that you may serve me; if you utter worthy, not worthless, words, you will be my spokesman.... I will make you a wall to this people, a fortified wall of bronze; they will fight against you but will not overcome you, for I am with you to rescue and save you,' declares the Lord" (Jeremiah 15:19-20).*

The words hit my ears. I immediately sat up and hurriedly opened the Bible. *"If you return... if you utter worthy, not worthless words, you will be my spokesman."* I kneeled and prayed earnestly that I would be able to obey without fear. Young-Gil always said, "Just as in a lab where you can only achieve good results when you follow the rules, let's follow God's rule that says, *"Therefore do not worry about tomorrow, for tomorrow will worry about itself. Each day has enough trouble of its own" (Matthew 6:34).* When we obey God's words, we will surely experience evidence that He lives."

It was very difficult for me to follow this rule. Absolute trust in God was not easy, but not believing in His word was the same as not believing in Him. In order to drive out my fears, I held on to a Bible verse that contained the key to pleasing God. *"Without faith it is impossible to please God, because anyone who comes to him must believe that he exists and that he rewards those who earnestly seek him" (Hebrews 11:6).* I cried out to the Lord that morning. God seemed to be saying, "If you build the school as if nothing is wrong, then I will use you as my spokesman!" Had not Young-Gil always said that his calling was to become a "voice" that cried out?

Buy the Field at Anathoth!

On our sinking ship in a storm, our most important compass was the word of God. We read Jeremiah 32 with desperate hearts, thinking that, perhaps, we would hear God commanding us to change directions.

Jeremiah was confined in the courtyard of the guard for having prophesied to Zedekiah, the king of Judah, that Judah would soon fall to the hands of Babylon and that its inhabitants would live as captives for 70 years. Jeremiah then heard the voice of God again. "Buy the field of your cousin Hanamel at Anathoth! You have the right to redeem it and possess it." While his country was being overrun and its people taken captive, God told Jeremiah, who was then in prison, to "buy a field." God wanted to show his people that He would restore Israel in 70 years, regardless of Jeremiah belief in God's promise. That must have been a truly difficult command to obey; buying a land when the country was going under with faith that it will be restored in 70 years.

Our situation was like Jeremiah's. We realized that God wanted us to believe that He himself would lead this university if its vision were to serve as a beacon to the next generation.

Faced with the daunting task of obeying the call to lead Handong, Young-Gil and I meditated on God's word again and again to hear His voice. *"Ah, Sovereign Lord, you have made the heavens and the earth by your great power and outstretched arm. Nothing is too hard for you" (Jeremiah 32:17).* The prayer that Jeremiah had offered with sadness in his heart was also our prayer.

The book of Jeremiah continued to feed us with God's voice. *"'I myself will gather the remnant of my flock out of all the countries where I have driven them and will bring them back to their pasture (Handong), where they (the students) will be fruitful and increase in number. I will place shepherds (the professors) over them who will tend them, and they will no longer be afraid or terrified, nor will any be missing,' declares the Lord" (Jeremiah 23:3-4). "Then this city (Handong) will bring me renown, joy, praise and honor before all nations on earth that hear of all the good things I do for it (the Handong students); and they will be in awe and will tremble at the abundant prosperity and peace I provide for it" (Jeremiah 33:9).*

Searching for the First Handong Faculty

Young-Gil said, "The most important task in starting a Christian university is to find faithful professors who excel academically and, at the same time, have a godly vision to serve their students. Fortunately, there are several faithful scientists at the Korea Association for Creation Research (KACR), and I hope that some of them will join me to work at Handong. God already prepared professors for the school."

Just as Young-Gil said, several colleagues at KACR agreed to come. *"I know, O Lord, that a man's life is not his own; it is not for man to direct his steps" (Jeremiah 10:23).* Some did not take long to decide; some hesitated. But everyone ultimately left their familiar surroundings with the confidence that God had invited them to begin a new work. *"But whatever was to my profit I now consider loss for the sake of Christ. What is more, I consider everything a loss compared to the surpassing greatness of knowing Christ Jesus my Lord" (Philippians 3:7-8).* Someone told us, "Until now I had been teaching as if knowledge and faith are unrelated. Now I can freely teach that Jesus is the Lord of all knowledge – how worthwhile and exciting!"

Time passed cold-heartedly, and in June 1994, before leaving for the United States on a trip for recruiting professors, Young-Gil met with Father Reuben Archer Torrey III at Jesus Abbey in the mountain of the eastern part of Korea. He gave Young-Gil precious and practical advice.

"In order for Handong to be a university based on pure Christian principles, the most important factor is the quality of the professors. You must recruit those who are well-qualified in all three areas; character, ability, and faith. The most important of the three, however, is character. If you only emphasize academic ability, then Handong will be no different than all other schools. The character of a professor is just as important as his faith. Faith without a fine character can easily lead to hypocrisy as with the Pharisees and the teachers of the law. Those with strength of character, even if they are beginning Christians, will be good role models for the students. Faith will mature as we live out our lives."

Young-Gil never forgot his advice. A man's character was revealed when his interests were at stake or during times of danger, and so his advice took on more meaning as time passed. Even Jesus' disciples picked those who were respected by men when they were called to select the seven deacons (Acts 6:3).

Dad and Dr. Kim are Both Abnormal

In the summer of 1994, the mountains and fields of Pohang were withering away in an unprecedented heat wave. There had not been any rain for almost two years, and the area was about to ration water supply. The fields were cracked like the back of a turtle. Handong's situation too was drying up like the ground. Young-Gil began his search for a Christian businessperson who could help Handong.

At that time, Dr. Y. Kim, a computer scientist in the United States, who had decided to join Handong, notified us that he would visit Korea for a few days. Should he visit in a situation like this? Would he really give up his 14 years of life in the United States and return to Korea? I asked Young-Gil, "Wouldn't it be better if he came after the financial situation improved?"

"God's people will not be shaken by circumstances. The man I saw was definitely a man of God. Let's wait and see," he replied. When Young-Gil returned from Pohang, I asked him, "Did you explain everything to Dr. Kim?"

"Yes, of course."

"What did he say?"

"Ask him, if you want to know yourself."

I asked Dr. Kim, who was sitting in our living room, "Dr. Kim, will you still come to Korea?"

"Mrs. Kim, how can God's work progress smoothly without prayers? Everything is God's signal for us to pray! I am coming."

His words gave us great courage. Neither Young-Gil who was excitedly talking about the school's vision despite the grave financial setback, nor the professor who was returning to Korea in spite of it, seemed normal. Our daughter Jong-Min, who had been listening to our conversation, took my hand and led me to our bedroom. She circled her finger on top of her head and said, "Both Dr. Kim and Dad are abnormal. But I think I now understand that **'faith is being sure of what we hope for and certain of what we do not see'" (Hebrew 11:1).**

Her eyes were twinkling with tears.

"My righteous one will live by faith. And if he shrinks back, I will not be pleased with him. But we are not of those who shrink back and are destroyed, but of those who believe and are saved" (Hebrews 10:38-39).

What is faith? Does faith requires us to take actions that supersede our common sense? It was truly challenging to act as if we had proof that God will accomplish His will and that we have already seen what we believe in the face of reality - a reality that we could not see with our eyes, neither feel with our hands nor hear with our ears. What if things do not work out as we go forward? That Sunday, Pastor Ha said during his message that "fear closes the door to the future." What was our fear? When I thought about it, our fear was the fear of failure. Our fear was unbelief.

The professors within Korea who had decided to join Handong were also unshaken. God called us as his tools, and he pushed us to take one step at a time. God did not allow us to see very far into our future. Had we known that countless trials and persecution were headed in our way, including prison, we might have turned away. *"Your word is a lamp to my feet and a light for my path" (Psalm 119:105).* God's words, "a lamp to my feet" and not a high beam, meant we could only see a few steps at a time.

Handong's First Gift, the Latest Computer

In July 1994, Young-Gil visited Dr. Y. Lee, the former chairman of TRIGEM Computer Company, and he explained to him in detail his vision of a new education at Handong.

"We plan to use English as a main teaching language, train computer platform to all students and teach Chinese to all freshmen students to better prepare them in the IT-driven global world. All exams will be conducted without supervision for honesty education." Dr. Y. Lee enthusiastically encouraged Young-Gil.

"Such a university is greatly needed at a time like this. Your idea is very forward-thinking. You're just as good as your elder brother!"

Dr. Lee and Young-Gil's elder brother, Ho-Gil, had a close friendship, which developed when they were classmates at Seoul National University majoring in physics. During the Korean War, when they both took refuge in Busan, a port city in the southeastern coast, they were filled with dreams for advancing their country's science and technology. These two poor college students would shout as they looked out on the vast Pacific ocean and the war-torn country, "Our fellow countrymen, wait for just a while longer! We will soon create a country of great living, one that we can all be proud of."

When they came back to Seoul after the war, they often skipped meals and walked instead of taking the bus to save money, but they never gave up their dreams.

Dr. Lee promised that he would donate 80 new computers to Handong right away. In September 1994, a truck arrived at school with the latest computers. The fact that the computers had arrived just in time for the Ministry of Education's pre-opening inspection was another sign from God that we needed to continue without giving up. Looking at all the computers unloaded in the information technology (IT) room, we forgot about our worries for a moment and became excited as we imagined all the students sitting in front of these new computers. The computers were recorded as the first donation to Handong. Since they had just come out on the market, Handong became the first university to use these latest model computers.

God's Hand behind Us

In order to open the school in time for the academic year of 1995, we needed to begin promotional activities in August 1994 at the latest. But we could not even consider such efforts. Then in early August, we received an unexpected news. Based on the results of Young-Gil's research at NASA, Young-Gil was listed in the 1994 American Men and Women of Science (AMWS).

I had secretly hoped that the name "Handong" would slowly disappear from people's minds, so that an escape would be easy. But contrary to my wishes, major newspapers introduced Young-Gil as the "designated president of Handong Global University." When I saw the articles, I felt that an invisible hand was putting handcuffs around our wrists. It was as if God were pushing us from behind not to waver but to press forward with the university.

Interviews by leading mass media magazine followed. Regardless of how the school's future would unfold, opportunities to promote it were handed to us. Thankfully, the reporters had a positive interest in the new university that the scientist Young-Gil Kim was to lead. It was probably because Korea's university system was so thirsty for a new type of education.

Young-Gil explained to the reporters, "Most of our country's university curricula are the same, but Handong Global University's vision is to offer a specialized, differentiated educational program that will raise elite workers who will not need re-education to become valuable to industries. To fulfill the requirements of twenty-first century globalization, we will invite native English-speaking professors so that our students can learn practical English that they can use in real life. We will require computer education for all students regardless of their majors, and we will tear down the walls between departments so that students can learn about broad related areas in their undergraduate education. Above all, Handong will educate its students based on the Christian faith, and our goal will be a holistic education that addresses our students' intellects, characters, and spirits."

The reporters listened intently to Young-Gil's confident introduction of Handong's vision, but I was apprehensive. How could he speak with such certainty? Where would he get the money to hire English professors and buy computers?

"Don't hesitate; just move forward!" I could feel God's intervention, but I was still nervous.

Korean Government Approves Opening of Handong

Young-Gil continued to desperately look for Christian business-person to take charge of the university, as if looking for a nanny to feed a motherless baby. Handong was in a thick fog, and we could not see even an inch ahead. Young-Gil and I could not sleep very well.

Most of all, we needed $3 million to make a deposit with the Ministry of Education in order to be approved by the Korean Government. The deadline was fast approaching. The needed amount would not solve all our problems, but we could not give up. *"I lift up my eyes to the hills – where does my help come from? My help comes from the Lord, the Maker of heaven and earth. He will not let your foot slip – he who watches over you will not slumber. The Lord will watch over your coming and going both now and forevermore" (Psalm 121:1-8).*

At that time, the early morning prayer service was held at Onnuri (All Nations) Presbyterian Church in Seoul in which Young-Gil was an elder. The church decided to support Handong with $90,000. Another church also readily loaned us $500,000 without interest. After much borrowing, we were finally able to make our deposit.

On December 4, 1994, the Ministry of Education gave its final approval to launch Handong Global University. Handong was now officially accredited as a four-year university in Korea. *"'Do I bring to the moment of birth and not give delivery?' says the Lord. 'Do I close up the womb when I bring to delivery?' says your God" (Isaiah 66:9).*

CHAPTER 4:

Building Handong: Laying the Cornerstone

President Kim, it is Nonsense!

The level of a newly chartered university is usually established by the caliber of the first entering students. Young-Gil and professors discussed what qualifications they would require of their first incoming students in order to accomplish Handong's educational ideal. Their conclusion was to admit those who scored in the top 25 percent of the National College Entrance Exam or whose GPA was in the top 15 percent of their class. Some professors strongly disagreed with such high criteria, stating that the school would not be able to recruit enough students. Even the government officer at the Ministry of Education was opposed to the idea.

"President Kim, it is a nonsense! Handong is a new university in the remote countryside. If you put such stringent limits on the applicants, you will not be able to fill your recruitment quota. Such qualification limits are also against the Ministry's policy of 'equal education for all.' As long as I hold my office, I will never allow it."

Young-Gil visited him several times and tried to convince him, but it was a dead end. Several staff members at school also questioned the feasibility of Young-Gil's plan. But Young-Gil believed that God would provide since He was the one who gave us the great vision in the first place. And so, he pushed forward with confidence. When we could no longer delay submitting our admissions criteria to the Ministry of Education, the official who had vehemently opposed our plan was suddenly transferred to an overseas post, leaving his office behind. God had surely heard the official's vow to reject our plan as long as he was in charge. *"You know when I sit and when I rise; you perceive my thoughts from afar. You discern my going out and my lying down; you are familiar with all my ways. Before a word is on my tongue you know it completely, O Lord" (Psalm 139:2-4).*

When Young-Gil visited the Ministry of Education again, the official temporarily in charge said, "The air of freedom and privatization these days is spreading even to the field of higher education. If you feel comfortable, try it your way!"

Our admission criteria were finally approved as a "legally allowable differentiation."

Effective Advertisement Strategy

The university entrance exam day was just around the corner when Young-Gil visited the Ministry of Education on December 20, 1994. A government official, who must have had a good impression of Young-Gil, approached him and said, "I was greatly moved by your vision for university education in the 21st century. If you want to effectively promote Handong, you should meet with the reporters. If you explain Handong's innovative vision and how it differs from the existing universities, I believe you will receive much positive media coverage. This is a high-level public relations strategy."

Extremely thankful for the suggestion, Young-Gil visited the pressroom to meet reporters covering education for various newspapers.

"Universities also have to become competitive in preparation for the new century, and they must focus all their resources on raising global leaders," Young-Gil said, "Universities must perform not only academic research, but also cultivate capable talents needed in the society of the 21ˢᵗ century. All students should have double major for a wide field of knowledge. To teach honesty, all exams at Handong will be conducted without supervisors, and social service and teamwork will be required. The existing universities in Korea all have curricula and educational content that are similar. We cannot expect improvement in the quality of our students nor can we aptly prepare them for the global community with standardized education. We urgently need to reform our university education."

The reporters listened attentively as the new university president passionately communicated his vision. The press meeting resulted in surprisingly positive coverage. The evening TV news and newspapers all reported Handong as a new university model that had limited its applicants' qualifications. The coverage caught the attention of many people. After an article, "A New University Model Unveiled," appeared prominently in a major daily newspaper, new phone lines had to be added in our admission offices.

The power of the media publicized Handong across the entire country, and we succeeded in our high-level PR strategy without spending a dime. Once again, we felt God's hand that had brought the maximum result through the best method in the minimum time. *"The Lord is with me; he is my helper" (Psalm 118:7).*

When Handong received official approval to open its doors, the school had less than a month to recruit students. The professors traveled in pairs to cities all over the country and visited every high schools, private tutoring centers, and church youth groups to promote Handong.

Traveling all over the country without a break, Young-Gil caught pneumonia and could no longer speak. Even after suffering through the night with a high fever, he left the house every morning with a thick scarf around his neck. All the professors spent their energies on recruiting new students. They were like the Israelites called to rebuild the fallen city walls. *"Your people will rebuild the ancient ruins and will raise up the age-old foundations; you will be called Repairer of Broken Walls, Restorer of Streets with Dwellings" (Isaiah 58:12).*

After an intense month, January 5, 1995, the day of registration, finally arrived. We started our day with excitement and nervousness like students waiting for their admission results. The sky looked heavy with clouds as if it was about to snow. Unable to find a proper venue in Seoul, we decided to receive the applications on the first floor of Onnuri Presbyterian Church. Beginning at 9 o'clock in the morning, students and their parents started streaming in through the church doors. They sat and talked with professors in the church café. The friendly, warm atmosphere substantially differed from the registration sites of other universities.

Amazing Admission Result

After three days of registration, the admissions results were finally announced. After only a month of promotional activities and despite the strict qualification criteria, 4,872 students had applied for 400 spots. The competition was more than 12:1. That evening, the national news hour was filled with stories about "the incredible admissions miracle at the new Handong Global University." It was indeed a true miracle.

In the midst of all media buzz, we were the most shocked of all. The high competition ratio was surprising, but even more shocking was the fact that the admitted students' average grades were around the top 5 percentile of the nation, on par with top-tier universities in Seoul which had decades of history to back up their reputations.

The applicants all had different stories. Many said that their high school teachers strongly opposed their choice, asking why a student with such high GPA would choose to attend a new provincial university. Some students' parents vehemently opposed them, while others submitted their applications because of strong pressure from their parents. There was even a small group of non-Christians who had nevertheless applied, as they were drawn to Handong's new approach to education. One pastor advised a student struggling to decide between a top-notch university in Seoul and Handong by saying, "Go to the big-name school if you want to be well-off for a little while, but go to Handong if you want to be well-off for eternity." *"A man can receive only what is given him from heaven"* *(John 3:27).*

Only the Servants who brought the Water Knew

A few days later, a graduate student from another University visited Handong and wanted to use Handong's admissions miracle as part of his research. Young-Gil explained Handong's secrets to him.

"I can explain to you about Handong's admission result with the story in Chapter 2 of the Gospel of John. At a lively wedding party, the hosts ran out of wine. Mary, who had been invited as a guest, quietly told Jesus about this perplexing situation, but a command was given to the servants that could not be understood with a logic or common sense. Jesus' command was to fill the jars with water and deliver the water instead of wine to the master of the banquet. It was a risk to follow a ridiculous order that could lead to a disaster, but the servants obeyed and did as Jesus commanded them.

When they did, the result was quite astonishing. Water turned into a higher quality wine than they had before! No one knew where this great wine had come from – neither the master of the banquet, nor the bride and groom. But the servants knew the secret: They knew that Jesus Christ was the one who had caused this transformation!

"Handong Global University was left without any financial support before it even opened its doors, just like the wedding banquet that ran out of wine. But we were the mere 'servants' who obeyed by applying the Bible to our situation. The main force behind Handong's miraculous admissions results was neither the president professors, nor the curriculum. The living God, Jesus Christ is the one who caused this unimaginable outcome! I believe God has plans to be carried out in our time through Handong. We are the servants called to this work. And secrets that only the servants know are being added every day."

The Opening Ceremony

March 7, 1995 was the day when the first page of Handong's history opened.

**Handong opened in 1995, in Pohang, Korea, with
outstanding 400 students, and in 2006 about 3,500
students from Korea and abroad (so far 58 nations).**

Students from all over the country came in waves, like young pioneers stepping onto the virgin soils of ancient lands. The campus was set in a wilderness of bitter ocean winds surrounded by hills and fields that had been frozen all winter long, but the school grounds, where the opening ceremony took place, were filled with warm sunlight. The faculty had worked through many nights preparing to receive the new family. The professors held early-morning prayer meetings at the school prayer room and awaited their first meeting with the students with excited hearts.

We celebrated three ceremonies that day: The opening of the school, the welcoming ceremony for the incoming students, and the inauguration of the school's first president. However, I sat with a deadly pale face. It was not because of the bitter wind of the Handong field in March. It was because of all the eyes of people who had placed futures at Handong – the eyes of the youthful, bright students; the parents full of hope and expectations; the faculty members and guests who congratulated us. We had given birth to a precious body after incredible delivery pains, but we had no idea as to how to raise the child. How could the wonderful blueprint of a new education that Young-Gil proclaimed come to life without financial backing? I shivered when the realization of all the responsibilities Young-Gil had to bear from then on finally hit me.

All of a sudden, clouds started to cover the sun filling the sky with gray darkness. Gusts of winds began to blow across the school grounds. Floral arrangements on the stage started collapsing one by one. The gusty winds threatened us as if they wanted to amplify the fears in my mind that made me frozen in my seat. We could no longer hear the words coming out of the loudspeakers. For a fleeting moment, I felt myself longing to return to the security of the previous place at KAIST. However, even that was only a brief moment and my mind went back to focus on the podium to follow the program.

On that Handong's inauguration ceremony of March 7, 1995, all Handong families, including the president, the professors, the staffs, and the parents together with the chartered class students, all entered the school in the wilderness, the school of suffering and prayers. Indeed, they were entering the school of the Holy Spirit, a blast furnace in which the raw ores would be turned into refined steel under an intense heat and fire. While they are in it, all vain thoughts, worldly desires and vanity would be burnt off and the residue would float as sludge; only the refined pure metal would be collected on the bottom as God's people. Handong is indeed "God's small school" that produces a few broken people that God needs, that had been featured in the book, "A Tale of Three Kings – A Study in Brokenness" by Gene Edwards (Tyndale House Publishers 1992). "God has a university. It's a small school. Few enroll; even fewer graduate. Very, very few indeed. God has this school because he does not have broken men and women. Instead, he has several other types of people. He has people who claim to have God's authority, and don't, people who claim to be broken, and aren't. And people who do have God's authority, but who are mad and unbroken. And he has, regretfully, a great mixture of everything in between. All of these he has in abundance, but broken men and women, hardly at all.

In God's sacred school of submission and brokenness, why are there so few students? Because all students in this school must suffer much pain. And as you might guess, it is often the unbroken rulers (whom God sovereignly picks) who metes out the pain. David was once a student in this school, and Saul was God's chosen way to crush David."

Handong Students Will Turn Korea Upside Down

Young-Gil had been searching for a foreign professor to teach English. He contacted Dr. Terry Spohn, a professor of biology at Liberty University in Virginia whom we had known through creation science activities. Since Young-Gil was hesitant to ask a biology professor to teach English, he asked Dr. Spohn to recommend English teachers who could come to Pohang. However, after listening to Young-Gil's plea for help, Dr. Spohn decided to take a sabbatical year for research and come to Handong.

In February 1995, Dr. Spohn arrived with his family in Pohang.

The first foreign professor Dr. Terry Sphon and his wife Kay chatting with the chartered class students in 1995.

His wife, Kay ,also taught English, and their two daughters, Christy, 15, and Sarah, 12, who were home-schooled, also served as diligent teacher's assistants. We thus ended up with four English teachers at once. These teenage girls with emerald eyes and blond hair energized the campus. Even the shy Korean students got along well with them.

Dr. Spohn suggested that each students have an English nickname. So, they came up with names like Jonathan, Michael Jordan, James Dean, Vivien Leigh, Richard Nixon, Nancy Reagan, David, and Joseph. Dr. Spohn joked, "There isn't a professor in the world who teaches so many famous people in one class!"

After a year at Handong, during which he witnessed some signs of unfortunate developments, he said as he departed, "President Kim! Do not give up the vision that God has given you, but endure with patience to the end even if things are difficult. The future leaders of Korea will pour out of Handong. I am sure of it. They will change Korea upside down!"

Peculiar Systems at a Peculiar School
Handong's Honor Code

With the vision of raising global leaders, who are capable and honest in front of God whom we cannot see and in front of people whom we can see, we decided to implement an honor code system of unsupervised exams. *"I the Lord search the heart and examine the mind, to reward a man according to his conduct, according to what his deeds deserve" (Jeremiah 17:10).* My daughter, Joann Jong-Min, was attending Bryn Mawr College in Pennsylvania which practiced an honor code. She sent a letter to the students of Handong as they prepared for the honor code:

To all the students at Handong:

I am a junior at Bryn Mawr College where we have an honor code system. As a Bryn Mawr student, I am proud to say that we are always following a higher moral standard. Bryn Mawr students are generally best known for their honesty and integrity.

The purpose of honor code system is to train every individual to be a mature being that takes responsibility for one's actions.

Therefore, our honor code system has two distinct areas – academic and social honor code. We have these two areas because we believe that the honor code is only successful when students form trust with one another not only academically but also socially. Only when there is a balance between the two areas, one can truly say that the honor code system is implemented properly.

If one witnesses a violation of the honor code, what should one do? First rule is that since the honor code is based on trust and respect, one should not discuss such situation with anyone who is not directly involved. Reporting a violation of any honor code should be confidential. If one witnessed a violation, one should confront the person in question with respect and advise him/her to inform the professor. If he/she does not take action in the next two or three days, then the witness need to step up and inform the professor and explain the situation. This is probably the hardest part, but if you let the situation go, then you too are violating the honor code by not being honest to yourself, and soon the honor code system will become meaningless.

One thing you must remember at all times is to respect others. School has a very competitive environment. We tend to compare ourselves to other peers, to see if one finished homework and to see what grades one received on the exam. Competition is what leads one to copy someone else's homework and to cheat on exams. Here at Bryn Mawr, we have an unspoken rule not to ask about each other's grades or the status of the homework. This is to avoid any situation that will give rise to competition. The honor code will be unfamiliar to you at first, but once you make it a part of your lives, all of you at Handong will be commended by God and others not only during your school years but also after graduation.

A school's traditions are founded by its first class of students. I believe that Jesus Christ will be pleased with your efforts to implement the honor code. I too will pray for Handong as it takes off with a new vision and dreams.

From Joann Jong-Min Kim

During the first mid-term exams at Handong, one professor said as he handed out the exams, "All of you today will take two tests.

One test is a test of honesty before God, and the other is a test of knowledge. God is present not only in churches, but also in our classrooms. I hope that you will do well on both tests."

When the professor left the classroom, the students' initial responses were varied. Some students were thrilled and said, "Hey, this is great! Cheating is a form of ability as well, so let me try my best!"

But most students said, "Unsupervised exams are definitely tempting. When there is a question that I know I studied but can't remember the answer, I want to look it up in my book. But I overcame the temptation when I realize that my conscience was more important than the exam."

Some students who had transferred to Handong from other schools were moved by the honor code.

"At the school that I attended before, the copy room during exam periods was filled with students making reduced copies. When so many students were cheating without guilt, I felt like I was losing out by taking the exams honestly."

Some reporters asked one of the professors, "What do you take pride in at Handong?"

"Undoubtedly, our honor code. One time, I returned exams, and told my students to let me know if I have graded any questions incorrectly. I said it because I was concerned that some grades may be too low. Then a couple of students came to see me. 'Professor, you gave me a grade that's too high. I gave the wrong answer, but you gave me full credit for it.' I was truly shocked."

In January 2000, six years after the institution of the honor code, the student government conducted a survey to the entire student body to see how this tradition has been passed on. Sixty percent of the respondents said that they were observing the honor code with a clear conscience before God. Twenty percent responded that they were tempted from time to time but that they had not erred. Sixteen percent responded that they had failed several times but had repented and were determined not to do it again. However, 4 percent responded that they had violated the honor code before and that they would continue to do so in the future.

Announcing the outcome of the survey, the student representative said to the parents, "You will be disappointed if you think that Handong students are extraordinary because of the honor code. Handong Global University is not the Garden of Eden. We have students among us who fail the honor code. The take-home exams are especially tempting, but despite those students who fall into temptation, we are still proud to be Handong students. Handong Global University is a battlefield where we are trained every day to become men and women of God. We do not want to criticize the 4 percent who do not follow the honor code. Rather, because of them, we are able to renew and reaffirm our commitment to be honest in the classroom."

From the fall of 2002, students declared an honor code week to strengthen Handong's tradition to live righteously before God and men. One professor, who had been with Handong since its inception, called for the revival of the honor code spirit of 1995.

"The year 1995 was a stupefying time for all of us at this school in the wilderness. Four hundred students and 20 professors created Handong's own culture from scratch. At that time, the two most common words at Handong were 'vision' and 'shock.' Students, who for nearly 20 years had been indoctrinated by secular culture and norms, were refreshingly shocked as they experienced new norms at Handong.

"The year 1995 laid the foundation for Handong's honor code. Although the school was poor and lacked educational supplies, love, respect and faith ran deep among students. We shared the feeling of 'you go, we go,' and hence, the honor code was launched. Without anyone pushing, each student voluntarily built it and promoted it. Based on such a tradition and history, the honor code became our identity, our living conscience before God. So dear students, let us arise again and pass on the honorable tradition that was started in 1995."

Handong's Promise Keeper

The male and female students at Handong live in separate buildings or wings in the dormitories, but most of the time they study, eat and enjoy each other's company. On campus, students make many good friends through healthy male-female relationships, and there are many "campus couples (CC)" as well.

What separates Handong from other campuses, however, is that Handong holds a promise keeper ceremony annually where students voluntarily pledge a covenant of purity before God. They promise to maintain physical purity before and after marriage, and a heart devoted to God for the rest of their lives.

The promise of sexual purity before marriage became a ceremony of holiness in which students make a commitment to be holy spiritually and physically as the bride of Jesus. *"Consecrate yourselves, for tomorrow the Lord will do amazing things among you" (Joshua 3:5).*

Teachers' Day

Korean schools celebrate Teachers' Day on May 15 every year to show respect and love to the teachers. On Teachers' Day in Handong, students cover their professors' office doors with colorful cards and decorations, and fill their offices with balloons. The professors at Handong feel fulfilled and happy as they see the offices that their students have cleaned and the cars that their students have washed. They smile brightly as they tell stories of how their students polish their shoes and "attack" their feet to give them foot massages.

Just recently, in May 2005, Young-Gil and I received an unforgettable Teachers' Day gift. About 400 alumni had joined together to buy a new car for us. Even alumni studying abroad contributed, and some students got an advance to join the move. Their gift had special meaning because of a story behind it.

One day in March 2005, on our way back to Pohang from a city in the southern part of Korea after a speaking engagement, Young-Gil's car suddenly broke down at a rest area on the highway. Ever since the car was purchased in 1997, the car was a good work house on which Young-Gil had been to all corners of the country, attending various speaking engagements and fund raising events for the school. The odometer of 370,000 km (231,250 miles) testified that the breakdown did not come as a surprise. The school had suggested purchasing a new car for some time, but Young-Gil had opposed it, considering the financial situation of the school. At the rest area, we were fortunate to catch a ride with a patrol car to return home.

A few Handong graduates learned of the incident, and the story had spread quietly among alumni. Some alumni decided to buy a new car for the president and started to pool money, and soon, others joined. Out of the 400 contributors, around 200 names were unfamiliar even to the Handong student government. I recognized a few of the alumni's names, students who had previously been half-hearted toward the school. The donation soon amounted to $25,000.

Then one alumnus, who was working for the Hyundai Motors, came up with an idea to make Young-Gil the first recipient of the latest Hyundai car model, the new Grandeur. The company's public relation office was deeply moved by the Handong alumni's love toward the school and their president, and agreed to discount the cost of the car to meet the amount they had collected.

When we received the first new Grandeur, Young-Gil said to the alumni and students, "I praise the God of all comfort! I wish to share this honor with all the faculty members, who have taught and served these students well. I am so proud of you. You have made a beautiful impact on this society, where the relationship between teachers and students has become weaker."

Students put their hands on the car, and gave a prayer for the car, "New car! Make sure you provide a comfortable and safe ride for our president!"

We Want a Cafe!

In May 1995, Young-Gil came home and said suddenly, "How much would it cost to open a café at the school?"

"Why a café all of a sudden?" I asked.

"This afternoon, some students came up to me and said, 'President Kim, we have nowhere to go other than our dorms and the library. We want a café where we can drink tea, listen to music, and talk with our friends.' So I said, 'Let's make one.'"

"How can we when we don't have any money?" I questioned.

The answer I got from Young-Gil was, "We need to pray to God!"

He gave me a newspaper article that he had cut out. It was an ad selling used sofas for $200. He said, "Go and see it tomorrow. We could buy a few sets with the money I have."

Young-Gil always felt sorry for the students, who hung around the lecture halls without having a place to sit and enjoy music and tea. He wanted to make their simple wish come true.

The next day, I visited the used furniture store in downtown Pohang with some professors' wives, but the sofas were so old that they looked ready to collapse. They did not seem to fit in our new building. We came outside, and I was saddened by the situation that forced us to look through the old furniture. We gazed up at the blue sky above.

"God, those sofas just won't do. Give us money to buy real furniture!"

Soon, the summer break began. The students would return at the end of the summer expecting a café. We had no money, and I was resentful that Young-Gil had given his word easily without the means to fulfill it.

I prayed to God with a desperate heart.

"God, you are a God who keeps all promises! Please do not let your son break his promise to his students! Give us the money to make a café!"

I had been worried about Young-Gil's credibility. It was a prayer to save Young-Gil's face rather than to glorify God. We had been reading the Book of Ruth at the time. Ruth had lost her husband at a young age. Instead of staying in her home country Moab where she could live comfortably, she followed her mother-in-law Naomi to Bethlehem. Her future was not guaranteed, but she went with a profession of faith that "your God is my God." But what awaited them was a severe famine. She began to glean fallen ears of grains in order to sustain herself.

I thought about how Ruth must have felt. How much her pride must have been hurt! How sad she must have been picking ears! Did she regret having followed her mother-in-law? One day, bags of grain were laid before her and Boaz was standing in front of her. *At this, she bowed down with her face to the ground. She exclaimed, "Why have I found such favor in your eyes that you notice me*

– a foreigner?" Boaz replied, "I've been told all about what you have done for your mother-in-law since the death of your husband – how you left your father and mother and your homeland and came to live with a people you did not know before. May the Lord repay you for what you have done. May you be richly rewarded by the Lord, the God of Israel, under whose wings you have come to take refuge." (Ruth 2:10-12). I cried as I read the Book of Ruth. From then on, I desperately prayed for a Boaz.

"God, you know well how we've come to be here today, but we cannot even provide a café for our students. Send us a Boaz as well!"

We decided to gather fallen ears of grains like Ruth, but I did not want to announce publicly that the school was poor. One professor, who had been discussing this with me, went to the choir room at Onnuri Presbyterian Church and said,

"If you have any sofas or furniture that you're not using but are too nice to throw away, please send them to our school. We need lots of furniture since we are a new school."

The choir members, who had been praying for Handong during the early morning service, decided to help. Soon afterwards, three trucks full of furniture arrived at the school.

We set the furniture in a clean, empty lecture hall putting the relatively newer furniture by the entrance. When we were finished arranging the room, Young-Gil called in students who were walking by.

"Come in – the café is ready!"

I was worried. What if the students are disappointed? As they looked around, the expressions on their faces were odd. Then, they bowed their head low and said, "President Kim, we are truly grateful to you. Thank you so much."

I could not bear to look straight into their faces. The room resembled a multi-colored, used-furniture warehouse. It could not have looked nice to the stylish young generation, but they understood our hearts that wanted to do something for them. People say that the children of poor parents appreciate their parents more!

Sometime later, I told this story to Pastor J. Yoo from Los Angeles, who had come to preach at the school chapel.

"God is steadfast yesterday, today, and throughout eternity. The God who sent Boaz to Ruth will also send a Boaz to Handong. I will pray as well."

He encouraged us. Sometime later, Pastor Yoo called us.

"Boaz has appeared! I will bring him to you."

A few days later, Pastor Yoo visited us with a young couple.

I recognized the wife right away. She was Mrs. Kang who had studied the Bible with me a few years ago, the wife of Mr. H. Kang, a member of Christian Business Men Committee (CBMC) in Seoul.

"Mrs. Kang! What are you doing here?"

I had always remembered her as a quiet and considerate lady.

"Mrs. Kim, you look pale and so much thinner!"

She must have read on my face all the hardships which we had gone through.

"Mrs. Kim, we were very much moved as we looked around the school. The students look so pure!"

Whenever I hear such comments, I feel inexpressible joy as I thank God for listening to our prayers. Sometimes, I raise my hands to the sky and offer a prayer of blessings upon the students of Handong, just like the high priests in the Old Testament.

"God, cover our Handong campus with the spirit of your holiness. Let them become young men and women who *"do not conform any longer to the pattern of this world, but [are] transformed by the renewing of [their minds]… able to test and approve what God's will is – his good, pleasing and perfect will"* (Romans 12:2). And cover Handong Global University with the spirit of Your glory. Let every person who visits the school feel Your presence."

Mrs. Kang said as she held my hands, "Mrs. Kim, make a café. We will help."

"Oh, God! How you answer our prayers! Thank you."

Mr. and Mrs. Kang had received an inheritance six months earlier when her father had passed away. They wanted to share some of their inheritance to help those in need, and Pastor Yoo happened to mention the need for a café at Handong.

Seeing them off at Pohang Airport, I wanted to ask how much they would be able to donate, but I could not bring myself to ask before we parted. A week later, we met them again in Seoul. After talking for a while, I could no longer hold back my curiosity and asked Mrs. Kang in a whisper, "How much will the donation be?"

"Mrs. Kim, it is $2 million."

I almost fell off the chair. I could not believe my ears. My heart beat rapidly in shock. Mr. and Mrs. Kang had initially decided to donate a portion of their inheritance, but their hearts swelled more and more as time went by. After listening to the story of Handong, her siblings decided to take part as well.

"With our inheritance, we could live more comfortably in a bigger house with a bigger car, but we decided to inherit our father's heart, which is far more valuable than his material inheritance."

As soon as they left, I told Young-Gil, "Do you know how much? It's $2 million! Two million! God has poured bags of grain in front of us that we cannot even count! He has sent us a Boaz at last!"

Young-Gil was in total amazement as well.

"Hallelujah! Praise God! But Young-Ae, I think we need to build a chapel first. A church needs to be built at God's university ahead of other things. Of course, we will also build a café. They should be arriving at their house by now, so let's call them."

Even though it was past midnight, Young-Gil pressed me to call. When I phoned them, they were in complete agreement. That was the moment when the chapel and the café were born simultaneously at Handong. That night, we could not sleep from all the excitement.

God's words are unshakable like *"firmly embedded nails"* *(Ecclesiastes 12:11),* steadfast without change, transcending time or people. We had been hoping for about $20,000. But God gave us $2,000,000 instead! How many times did God provide beyond what we had expected? God knew our need better than we did, and had prepared a provision for us far beyond our expectations.

The students returned after the summer break. Young-Gil wanted to spread the news to the students as soon as possible. Thankfully, Mr. and Mrs. Kang proceeded with the donation in a speedy manner. In early September during chapel, Mr. Kang stood in front of the students with Mr. D. Choe, an architect. Mr. Kang said, "Dear students, I envy all of you who attend Handong, where you are taught the spirit of Christianity. I was a member of a Christian student group during my university years, but I never read the Bible. If I had read the Bible even once, my life might be different now. I accepted Christ as my Lord and Savior just a few years ago. Mr. D. Choe, who stands here next to me, invited me to CBMC meeting where I restarted my walk of faith. The guest speaker that day at CBMC was your President Young-Gil Kim. Today, that three people are standing here. How incredible that we should meet here again like this! God's providence has no coincidence and is truly amazing."

Based on the pen name of Mrs. Kang's father, we decided to name the chapel 'Hyoam Chapel.' *"Yet it was good of you to share in my troubles.... I am amply supplied, now that I have received... the gifts you sent. They are a fragrant offering, an acceptable sacrifice, pleasing to God. And my God will meet all your needs according to his glorious riches in Christ Jesus" (Philippians 4:14-19).*

CHAPTER 5:

The Invisible War Begins

$2 Million Used in an Unexpected Way

After the death of Young-Gil's elder brother and his mother, his younger sister and his father also passed away in succession. Like Job, we lost four family members in a year's time. While we were in mourning for Young-Gil's father, another piece of shocking news came to us from one of the Handong's staff member.

"President Kim, we have a promissory note of $2 million due at the end of October 1995. If we do not pay, the school will go under."

At that time, some voices that wanted to turn the financially troubled HGU into a public community university began to emerge. If Handong were to become a municipal school, then we would no longer be able to protect its identity as "God's university," let alone the future of 400 students who had given up other prestigious schools with the sole purpose of attending God's university. Until then, Young-Gil's knowledge on the status of the school's finances was limited at best because financial matters were taken care by the Board of Trustees. However, as the board could not fill the role, Young-Gil himself had to protect Handong's identity from then on and carry the heavy burden of providing for the school's finances.

When autumn arrived, flowers bloomed all over the campus, but we had no time to enjoy the nature's beauty. As time passed, Young-Gil's heart was heavy with the urgency to build a new dormitory for students entering in 1996. The days were getting shorter, but the school had no money with which to build a new building. Young-Gil could not sleep most nights.

Then one day, he said decisively that he would begin construction believing in God, who is the Lord over gold and silver. Fear filled my thoughts as I predicted the difficulty Young-Gil might face if he did not pay the construction bills on time. Thus, began another adventure of following the path unseen. The construction company which took charge of the construction work told us that the building would not be ready in time for the incoming students next March because of the late start. On top of that, the deadline for the $2 million note, which we had no means to pay, was approaching fast. Young-Gil's distress deepened daily. One day, he said with a resigned voice, "Today was the deadline for the note, and we used Hyoam Chapel's $2 million as collateral to borrow $1.8 million and barely held off the note."

I cried in despair, "We've done wrong to Mrs. Kang and her family. There are so many people who want to turn Handong into a community school. What will they say now that the funds donated for the school's chapel are gone?"

Young-Gil responded to my outcry in sorrow, "There was no other way. If you react like this, I will go crazy."

I was taken aback by his words. Only then did I realize that Young-Gil was in a worse agony than I was. I withheld my tears. A while later, he said, "Our living God will neither allow Handong to go bankrupt nor allow government-sent directors to take over."

When Mr. and Mrs. Kang heard that their donation of $2 million had been used in an unexpected way, they encouraged Young-Gil instead.

"President Kim! Don't worry so much. We offered the money to God to be used for the school. If we had kept that money in a bank until construction began, the interest alone would have been significant. The fact that we transferred the money so quickly must have been for this purpose. When we first went to Pohang, my wife saw Mrs. Kim's thin face and pressed me to send the money as soon as possible, saying 'Why would they choose to suffer so much given all that they had before at KAIST?'"

When we thought about all that had happened, it was truly amazing that the donation for the chapel and the amount of the promissory note were exactly the same. The $2 million proved to be God's preparation for the events that were out of our control. But problems arose from another unexpected place. A local newspaper reported, "President Young-Gil Kim embezzled $2 million of donated funds." It was the signal flare for the upcoming war of prosecutions.

Pray for a New Chairman of Board

In October 1995, the founder of the Sunlin Good Samaritan Hospital, Dr. J. Kim, was recommended to become the second chairman of the board. But he called Young-Gil and said that he could not accept the position. We were very disappointed to hear his decision just two days before the planned board meeting. On the same day, our driver had also been in a traffic accident. We were very discouraged. Young-Gil and I sat with blank faces for a long time.

We prayed again for a new chairman. The only one we could ask was Pastor Ha, senior pastor of Onnuri (All Nations) Presbyterian Church, which we have attended since 1984. We called him. It was 11 pm.

"Pastor Ha, this is an important issue that will determine the future of Handong. Please agree to become the chairman of the board and protect the Christian identity of Handong. You have to decide until tomorrow."

Pastor Ha said that he will pray for Handong. The school was at crossroads and me. We could not sleep. After staying up through the night, we went to the school's prayer room at dawn. The familiar scenery seemed foreign under the car's headlights. The villages and fields surrounding the school were still asleep. The lights in the dormitories were off. Our students were peacefully sleeping in those buildings. How could they know, deep in their sleep, the distress that caused us to come running to the prayer room to cry out at this early dawn! We raised our hands in the dark room and prayed to God in tears. We cried out, "Our Lord, please send the person according to your plan. If pastor Ha is the person for the new chairman of the board for Handong, help him to decide!"

In the morning, the phone rang. It was the bright voice of Pastor Ha. He said,

"God must have heard your desperate prayers. A businessman has promised to help the school financially. Therefore, I will accept to become chairman of the board of Handong if the board of trustee approves it."

The board meeting was held and Pastor Ha was elected as the second chairman of the board for Handong. (However, the businessman did not keep his promise, and Pastor Ha and Handong had to face a serious financial difficulty later on.)

"This is what the Lord, the God of your father David, says: I have heard your prayer and seen your tears" (II Kings 20:5).

The Beginning of the Litigation Wars

Deadlines for promissory notes began to arrive in droves. Young-Gil lived attached to his phone. After obtaining a month's extension on $1.6 million to the construction company who built the dormitory, we received a call from that company just a few hours before the banks closed for the day. If we did not prepare $1.6 million in two hours, the school would go into the first round of bankruptcy. This meant that a government-appointed trustee would be dispatched.

In an unexpected turn of events, Pastor Ha and Young-Gil found out that a $1 million deposit that they had prepared for the Ministry of Education was still in the school's bank account. It was yet another coincidence that the account was in the same bank to which we needed to pay the promissory note. We needed the approval of the board and the Ministry of Education before using the funds for the purpose, but we decided to get approval afterwards and use the money right away, given the urgency of the situation. Even then, we had to come up with the remaining $600,000. At that moment, Pastor Ha remembered a phone call that he had received earlier from a businessman in the United States who had said,

"Pastor Ha, you have become the chairman of a new university, which is a position of great responsibility. I have some money saved in Korea to fund a new business, but I can let you use it for a month without interest. So please let me know if you need it."

The next day we were able to cover the $1.6 million note, but the news spread that Handong was about to declare bankruptcy. Pastor Ha and Young-Gil were indicted again for using the deposit without the approval of the board. Some people insulted us saying, "A penniless president is trying to create God's university." *"When Sanballat heard that we were rebuilding the wall, he became angry and was greatly incensed. He ridiculed the Jews, and in the presence of his associates and the army of Samaria, he said, "What are those feeble Jews doing? Will they restore their wall? Will they offer sacrifices? Will they finish in a day? Can they bring the stones back to life from those heaps of rubble – burned as they are?" Tobiah the Ammonite, who was at his side, said, "What they are building – if even a fox climbed up on it, he would break down their wall of stones!" (Nehemiah 4:1-3).*

Onnuri Church under Attack

The arrow then began to point at Pastor Ha of the Onnuri Presbyterian Church, who was the second chairman of the board of trustee of Handong from 1995 to 1996. A strange letter from "An Organization of Believers Who Love Onnuri Church" was delivered to every church member's house. Eleven blackmail letters denouncing Pastor Ha were sent to all the pastors and elders across the country. Letters slandering Young-Gil and Handong were also delivered to relevant government agencies and local households.

Ultimately, Pastor Ha was also summoned to the prosecutor's office. Unseen forces used many means to attack, but Pastor Ha and Young-Gil remained silent. Just like the early churches in Acts, which underwent revival as they were persecuted, Onnuri Presbyterian Church experienced intensified prayers at the early morning services. *"Then Asa called to the Lord his God and said, 'Lord, there is no one like you to help the powerless against the mighty. Help us, O Lord our God, for we rely on you, and in your name we have come against this vast army. O Lord, you are our God; do not let man prevail against you" (II Chronicles 14:11).*

In December 1995, Pastor Ha spoke with gravity at the church's board meeting. "I am confident that Handong Global University is a school that God has founded, and I believe that helping Handong will please God. Handong is in financial distress, and they need help now. Wouldn't our help be most worthwhile if we can give it when it is needed the most?"

After many meetings, Onnuri Presbyterian Church decided to take on the burden of a considerable portion of Handong's debt. I breathed a sigh of relief, but my heart was greatly distressed.

Young-Gil said to me, "Haven't we seen countless examples that proved God's presence at Handong? We will soon see the day when the graduates of Handong display their influence, for our country needs respectful leaders. Buildings become old and useless after several decades, but even a single leader of excellence can make a whole nation upright. Handong's mission is to train and raise God's people in Korea and abroad. They will serve in all areas of society for the future of our country and the world.

"When we look at the world history of education, including that of the United States, we see that many churches founded Christian schools and proactively supported them. As a result, Christian schools were able to stay true to their Christian identity and not become secularized. It is unfortunate that churches nowadays cannot do that. Most Christian schools increase enrollment in order to bring in tuition as their main source of finances. Consequently, they neglect educating their students as well-rounded people. The easiest way to address a school's financial needs is to increase the enrollment, but I believe a true education, one that raises students as whole men and women, is more important than a school's management. Onnuri Church has helped Handong and has shown us a new model of normalizing Christian education in Korea."

Pastor Ha marveled at Young-Gil, who was always so full of assurance, "President Kim, you seem to forget all the difficulties and remember only the positive things. Surely you are one of the people I know with the healthiest self-esteem."

God Repays!

When the construction of the second dormitory could not be completed in time for the students' arrival, the school decided to build new guesthouses for the international professors. The steel-framed buildings could be completed in two months and be used as temporary dormitories for the students for a semester. Mr. S. Lee, an elder at Onnuri Presbyterian Church, took on the design work for free.

But the approval for the construction from the city was delayed. If we excluded the holidays at the end of the year, our schedule would be extremely tight. Having no other alternative, the school began leveling the ground. As a consequence, Pastor Ha and Mr. Lee were prosecuted for violating construction laws. Mr. Lee was suspended from work for a month, and Pastor Ha had to pay a fine, but Mr. Lee encouraged us.

"President Kim, don't worry at all. There won't be any damage to my company. Strangely, we were flooded with work just before being suspended, and so we spent a very busy month. God must have known in advance. And in the meantime, we also won a big contract."

After these incidents, we managed to complete the guesthouse construction in time. The guesthouses stood on a hill across the engineering school, and they lacked neither in structure nor in design.

The incoming students who arrived at the guesthouses were happy that they got to live in new dormitories. But despite all our efforts, we still did not have enough rooms. We decided to temporarily remodel the second floor of the student's union building and use it as a dormitory. But because of this, Young-Gil was prosecuted again.

CHAPTER 6:

Marching Through Adversity

Never Give up!

The time for our second welcoming ceremony for incoming students arrived in March 1996. Our feelings were quite different from the previous year. The guest speaker, Rev. S. Kim, senior pastor of a Methodist church in Seoul, held up two pieces of paper, one that he crumpled in his hands and other that he folded carefully.

"I am one of the people who was most overjoyed to hear about Handong's basic educational philosophy and program. Look carefully at the crumpled piece of paper and the carefully folded piece of paper. The latter has plenty of space that can be used. The Bible tells us, *"The fear of the Lord is the beginning of knowledge, but fools despise wisdom and discipline" (Proverbs 1:7)*. Academia that does not acknowledge God who is the 'origin of knowledge' is like this piece of crumpled paper. Knowledge that is not based on the right set of principles can actually be harmful. All of you must first ask yourselves the fundamental question: 'For what purpose am I pursuing academics?' It is hard to find a university that teaches you the true purpose of academics and the right value system, but Handong Global University is different. You will find the answers here as you pursue your studies. You have chosen wisely. Never give up. God is with Handong Global University. Never ever give up!"

President! There is no Water!

A group of local people was hostile to the spirit of Handong. The opposition party of Handong raised two objections. The first was that Handong was overly Christian and therefore, had degenerated into a missionary training school. Some local residents were strongly antagonistic to the establishment of a genuine Christian university in the city of Pohang. These people insisted that Handong should be converted to a public community college.

The second opposition was that the citizens of Pohang did not receive any benefits from the school although it was located in Pohang. They wanted to change Handong into a large university with an enrollment of at least 10,000, so that local students can be admitted into Handong easily. Their demand was like a push to turn a newborn baby into a full-grown adult overnight. Young-Gil predicted that in a few years, there would be a large discrepancy between the total enrollment capacity at universities across Korea and the total number of prospective students due to the slow population growth. This would inevitably cause under-enrollment, especially at regional universities.

A group of opponents made a public statement charging that Young-Gil had sided with a genuine Christian education at Handong. They pursued Young-Gil's resignation from the presidency by initiating a petition in the streets and houses of Pohang city. *"Pharaoh and his officials changed their minds about them and said, "What have we done? We have let the Israelites go and have lost their services!" So he had his chariot made ready and took his army with him. He took six hundred of the best chariots, along with all the other chariots of Egypt, with officers over all of them"* *(Exodus 14:5-7).*

The atmosphere within the school was also becoming hostile to Young-Gil. Some voices began to mimic those from the outside. At last, in the third week of March in 1996, the lobby of the main school building was occupied by a group of opponents, and the peaceful campus soon turned into a battlefield. On March 20, 1996, after the second welcoming ceremony for incoming students, a phone rang early in the morning at our residence from the head of the school administration.

"President Kim, we have a serious problem. There has been no running water at the school since last night. It looks like an intentional disturbance acted by unknown people. There is no electricity, either. We have to prepare breakfast for more than 800 students, but we were able to make for only 150."

As he hung up the phone, Young-Gil's face was downcast. The dormitory where all the students were living had neither electricity nor running water.

"I can bear any hardship for myself, but not the students...."

He could not continue to speak. Tears flowed down on his face as he stood by the window. The sea glistened in the sunlight, seemingly uninterested. Even when he had stood at the crossroads of deciding whether or not to open the school, and in the face of the relentless personal attacks against him, Young-Gil had never seemed this pained. But in the face of the difficulties befalling his beloved, innocent students, he shed large, silent tears. He ignored breakfast and left the house for school. Breakfast could not be in his thoughts when his students had nothing to eat.

When he arrived at the school, the powerhouse, where the water supply, heating, and electrical facility was handled, was at a standstill. Only a professional engineer could determine the cause of the problem, and it did not seem possible to restore all the equipment without the responsible engineers. Young-Gil was told that even the engineering professors would need much time before being able to figure out the problem.

Bread and milk were distributed to the students for breakfast, and an emergency water truck was brought in to cook noodles for lunch. Bottled water was put in the students' rooms for drinking. However, the stench coming out of bathrooms into the hallways and lecture rooms foretold of the upcoming difficulty.

Despite their waterless morning, the students were unshaken and they headed for their classrooms according to schedule. Professors also continued with their lectures as usual. The engineering professors concentrated all their efforts on restoring the water supply. A miserable day was nearing its end. Young-Gil called in an anguished voice, "I think we need to find the company that installed the original equipment. Let us pray that we will find them."

At that moment, I suddenly remembered someone I met at a church in Pohang when I was invited there as a guest speaker. A man came up to me and said, "You are President Kim's wife, right? It's nice to meet you. You must be heart-broken over all the difficulties facing the school right now. It hurts to see President Kim suffering like this."

Greeting me warmly, he continued to speak.

"Mrs. Kim, I'm somewhat related to Handong as well. I am the president of the Korean operations for a Dutch waterworks company. Two years ago, we installed the water system at Handong. We worked extra hard to install the underground water tanks with care. You shouldn't have anything to worry about, even in severe droughts."

I remembered his face, but I could not recall his name. I did not know how I could locate him now, but I remembered a third person who stood next to us when we were talking. With her help, we were able to trace the man and get in touch with him whose name turned out to be Mr. H. Chung. However, it was well past 11 pm.

"It is too late today, so we would appreciate if you could help us tomorrow," I said to him.

"President Kim, I will be there right away. How can I wait when the students are in such a discomfort right now?"

Close to midnight, I went to school with one of the professors who lived in the neighborhood. Light rain was falling as we headed toward the school. The wet asphalt shone in the headlights. How could the school have ended up in this predicament? My eyes were tearing up. Wanting to avoid being noticed by those who opposed the school, the professor drove slowly with just the parking lights on. The darkness seemed to swallow up all our fears.

Mr. Chung had already arrived and had gone inside the power-house. As we waited for him anxiously, two dark shadows suddenly appeared out of the corner and walked toward us. We held our breath and looked at the two figures. Who could they be in the middle of the night? When the shadows noticed us, they too were startled.

"Mrs. Kim! Professor! What are you doing here in the middle of the night?" They were students.

"What are *you* doing here?" I asked.

"We were going to the hill, because we needed to, uhm, go to the bathroom. We will go somewhere else."

They were holding toilet paper in their hands. All the tears that I was holding back poured out of my eyes all at once. I felt so terrible but thankful at the same time for the students who were silently patient through the ordeal.

After a long while, Mr. Chung came out of the powerhouse and said, "We will have to call a professional mechanic tomorrow. There isn't a drop of water in the water tanks. It seems like no water has been going into the water tanks for a few days. It'll take some time to fill up the water tanks and purify the water."

The next day, Young-Gil made the announcement to the students.

"A most unfortunate problem has occurred on our campus, causing much difficulty for you students. The new students must have been especially shocked! I as the President will take any measures necessary to resolve the problem. It breaks my heart to see you suffer like this."

He began to choke up and could not continue. The students began to sob as well. My heart ached for my husband and the students, but the students actually arose to encourage Young-Gil.

"President Kim, we do not want anything to happen to you! We can endure this."

The first disaster area due to the water shortage was the bathrooms. After two days of no water, an unpleasant smell began to spread throughout the campus. The toilets in all the buildings on campus were full. The foreign professors were worried about the spread of infectious diseases, and the students, who were always friendly and talkative in the hallway were now silent, greeting us with only a bow.

"Hey, are you all mute now?"

"If we open our mouths, the smell of the bathrooms comes in. That is why we keep our mouths closed."

Among the students, bathroom secrets were circulating fast.

"Which bathroom on which floor is relatively less full?"

"The one on such-and-such a floor is still usable. By the way, when you go, make sure you use it at the right angle."

Some of the students rode their bicycles to a nearby town to wash themselves. Some of the townspeople were kind enough to provide them with warm water, saying that March was still too chilly for cold water. Some students brushed their teeth with soda pop, and nearby public baths overflowed with Handong female students.

The next morning, Mr. Chung came with the mechanics. That afternoon, the engines in the powerhouse finally began to turn, and sounds of water flowing from the water supply could be heard. Sometime later, water gushed out from the dried-up faucets. Professors and students who had been watching near the powerhouse yelled out loud cheers of happiness. It had been exactly thirty-six hours since the stoppage. Just as water flowed when Moses hit the stone for the Israelites suffering in the desert without any water, so water began to flow in the desert of Handong as well. My meeting with Mr. Chung two weeks before the water crisis was not a coincidence but in fact the workings of our Jehovah. *"Our help is in the name of the Lord, the Maker of heaven and earth" (Psalm 124:8).*

Students Became Watchmen

The water crisis became the impetus requiring an "emergency measure" at the school. A legal sanction was implemented that prevented any gathering or activity that might interfere with the students' studies. For the first time in a long while, we had peace on campus. The students took up brooms and mops to take down all the posters posted by the opposition group.

Professors and students majoring in the Mechanical and Control System Engineering program decided to guard the powerhouse in teams, fearing that a similar crisis might reoccur. Professors regularly stopped by the powerhouse to teach students the principles behind how the equipment worked. The students were busy studying for their classes and, at the same time, managing the school utility equipment. Young-Gil stopped by the powerhouse several times a day to encourage the students.

"Thank you for all your efforts. It's a hard work, isn't it?"

"President Kim! Don't worry about us. It's actually quite fun. We're practicing in advance what we'll learn in our third-year classes. We feel gratified knowing that our friends are getting hot water and sleeping in heated dorm rooms because of our efforts."

Just as Nehemiah held a plow in one hand and a weapon in the other in defense as he rebuilt the fallen walls of Jerusalem, so our professors and students overcame obstacles together with one heart. *"But we prayed to our God and posted a guard day and night to meet this threat.... Don't be afraid of them. Remember the Lord, who is great and awesome, and fight for your brothers, your sons and your daughters, your wives and your homes.... Those who carried materials did their work with one hand and held a weapon in the other.... They can serve us as guards by night and workmen by day" (Nehemiah 4:9-22).*

The Birth of the Parent Prayer Circle

After the news of the water crisis spread, parents from all over the country gathered at the school one day. Having received letters from unknown senders who attacked the school, they did not think that it was unusual for a university founded in the name of God to experience persecution. One parent encouraged us with the Word. *"Blessed are those who are persecuted because of righteousness, for theirs is the kingdom of heaven. Blessed are you when people insult you, persecute you and falsely say all kinds of evil against you because of me. Rejoice and be glad, because great is your reward in heaven, for in the same way they persecuted the prophets who were before you" (Matthew 5:10-12).*

Another parent asked Young-Gil, "President Kim, no matter how difficult things get for the school and no matter how much you are attacked, you wouldn't abandon the students here and walk away, would you?"

"How can I leave on my own without God's permission?"

The parents gave Young-Gil a standing ovation in tears. Young-Gil wiped away his tears with his shirtsleeve, like a small child. Inspired by the water crisis, more than 90 Parent Prayer Circles were born throughout the country. The parents decided to pray for the school where their precious children were, just as the Word tells us that *"where your treasure is, there your heart will be also" (Matthew 6:21).* I don't think there are many universities in the world that have parents praying in groups for the school and its president that he may not tire and fall. We are proud that we have received an inheritance from God that can *"never perish, spoil, or fade" (I Peter 1:4)*. We gained new strength from the knowledge that we have companions in the wilderness through the blood of Jesus Christ, which is thicker than the bond of human blood. The ship of Handong sailed ahead even faster because of the torrential winds around it. *"So in Christ we who are many form one body, and each member belongs to all the others" (Romans 12:5)*.

Severe Attack

Few days before a board meeting in March 1996, there were threatening signs. Rumors circulated that some people were about to make a hostile visit to the school. The target of attack, as always, was Young-Gil. The sky over the east coast was heavy with dark clouds.

"God, something frightening may happen today. Please send us a heavy rain!"

I prayed desperately for a rain. It was not just to relieve the land, which was suffering from a winter drought. I felt that a rain would be a sign that God was on our side. *"If calamity comes upon us, whether the sword of judgment, or plague or famine, we will stand in your presence before this temple that bears your Name and will cry out to you in our distress, and you will hear us and save us…. We have no power to face this vast army that is attacking us. We do not know what to do, but our eyes are upon you" (II Chronicles 20:9-12)*.

Drizzling rain in the morning slowly turned into thick streams of water, and soon torrential rain was pouring down from the sky. "God! You are on our side! Thank you Lord!" When Chairman Ha and Young-Gil were about to head for the school for the board meeting, the phone rang.

"President Kim, many unfamiliar people have started to gather at the school. Things seem out of place. Don't ride your car to school, but take your driver's Jeep instead."

The rain was getting heavier and pounding the ground relentlessly. Standing in the torrential rain, uninvited men were blocking the school entrance and communicating with each other with walkie-talkies. They could not identify the people inside the car because of the heavy rain. The Jeep went around the dormitory to the rear entrance of the main building. Strangers were guarding the front entrance, waiting for the President and the Chairman to show up. The two of them slipped safely through the west entrance to their offices. The atmosphere near the front entrance became increasingly frightening as time passed.

Around 2 pm, students began to gather at the main building and sit in hallways and stairways. They assembled themselves to form a human barricade. They said they had come up with a strategy in their dorms the night before. They had chosen a leader for each area. Those who were confident that they would stay calm and not respond in anger were stationed in the front, and they promised each other that they would exercise self-control and practice "take the blow if they were hit," and "smile even if they were cursed." The new incoming students were placed in the lobby.

Buses full of people arrived from downtown. They rushed into the main building. The men standing guard at the gate also came in. They began to speak to the students in rough language.

"Why are you bastards from Seoul here pretending to own this place?"

"Sir, this is our school. What do you want?"

"What? This isn't a school! This is a bunch of Jesus fanatics!"

They pointed at the students with their umbrellas and threatened them. If student in the front got excited in the face of continuing insults, then the one behind pulled him toward the back. The students' attitudes were truly mature and heart-breaking. The professors who were watching the scene tried their best to control their feelings as well. The atmosphere darkened more and more. People yelled out curses. The lobby turned into chaos with people trying to break into the meeting room and students trying to stop them.

At that moment, one student began to sing a hymn, and others soon joined in.

He is our peace
He has broken down every wall
He is our peace; He is our peace.
Cast all your cares on Him, for He cares for you
He is our peace; He is our peace

The students did not confront the hostile intruders. One freshman kneeled outside in the rain and started to pray. We wondered what the freshmen, who had just celebrated their welcoming ceremony, were thinking. The crowd that invaded the administration office yelled and demanded that the President show himself right away. When Young-Gil came out to the hallway, the students immediately made a passageway and cried out his name as if cheering an athlete.

"Young-Gil Kim! Young-Gil Kim!"

The sound brought tears to our eyes.

"But when Sanballat, Tobiah, the Arabs, the Ammonites and the men of Ashdod heard that the repairs to Jerusalem's walls had gone ahead and that the gaps were being closed, they were very angry. They all plotted together to come and fight against Jerusalem and stir up trouble against it" (Nehemiah 4:7-8).

Lord on my Side

A few days later, a reporter from a TV station came to the school without an advance notice. They said that they had come to follow up on a tip that President Young-Gil Kim had hired professors in return for bribes and that he had crippled the school's management with his religious bias. Although Young-Gil provided enough information to convince them that he was accused falsely, they appeared unwilling to correct their preconception.

After they left, the opponents from the city posted advertising banners all over Pohang with the TV program information that promised to expose the Handong scandal.

Regardless of truth, if this biased program were aired, the reputation of Handong and its President would be tarnished. And what a shock it would be to our students? I shook with fear. God, please rescue us! *"Hear me, O God, as I voice my complaint; protect my life from the threat of the enemy. Hide me from the conspiracy of the wicked, from that noisy crowd of evildoers" (Psalm 64:1-2).* I claimed the words of Psalm 64.

Then, I suddenly remembered someone from the distant past. Nine years ago, a producer from the same broadcast company named Mr. Y. Kim had visited Young-Gil at his KAIST office.

"Our KBS TV wants to produce a special program featuring you, Dr. Kim," he had said, "We want to tell the story of how you came from a remote village to become a NASA scientist and professor at KAIST. 'The Backwoods Mountain and the High-Tech Scientist,' will be broadcast on New Year's Day of 1987. You invented the country's first high-tech export item, a new semiconductor lead-frame material that was exported to Germany, and you've developed an alloy that leading semiconductor companies such as Motorola are using today. Your story will give our people pride and dreams. Please agree to participate in this program."

Young-Gil refused at first. "I have nothing to boast about. The fruits of my research do not come from my own capabilities. The success belongs to the excellent students of KAIST, the great research environment, and above all to God who has granted me wisdom."

The producer, however, would not relent and continued to press him. Young-Gil suggested a condition in return.

"If you promise to let your program reflect that I, as a Christian scientist, was able to produce these successful research results because of the wisdom that God gave me, then I will cooperate."

"No problem. We will portray your faith in our program."

Later, a crew visited the KAIST research lab, his hometown, his elementary school, and the factory where the copper alloy semiconductor material lead-frame had been produced. During the filming, we became friends with Mr. Y. Kim. We remembered for a long time afterwards his objective yet warm personality. In this moment of desperation, I remembered his name.

"Young-Gil, let's look for Mr. Y. Kim. I think he can help us."

"How can we find him now? We don't even know if he still works there. Let's pray that God will find him."

In three days, the program that slandered Handong was going to be broadcasted throughout the country. We hardly had the peace of mind to look for him at that time. The only thing that we could do was to pray. On that very afternoon, three days before the airing of the program, Young-Gil called me at home.

"Young-Ae, God has found the man that we were looking for! I'll tell you the details when I get home."

I breathed a sigh of thanks and relief. When Young-Gil came home, he told me that his secretary passed him a memo during a meeting that read "President Kim, please call me. Y. Kim from KBS TV." Young-Gil called him immediately.

"President Kim, do you remember me? I was looking at the footage on Handong today and was extremely shocked. You were being introduced queerly. The Dr. Kim that I know isn't that kind of a person, and I called because I want to know what is going on."

He turned out to be the leading producer of that program. It was yet another incredible coincidence. He told us that he asked his crew if there had been any bias during the filming, and his crew admitted that the story was somewhat one-sided. Young-Gil then explained our situation to him.

After listening to Young-Gil, he remarked, "A TV station empowered with the public's confidence cannot broadcast a program based merely on a tip. We would have made a grave mistake if I had not known your character."

And so the accusers' expectations were crushed. I was thankful that the ethics of the country's media were still functioning. I realized that there is not a single relationship that is not valuable in some way. The countless threads of relationships we encounter in our lives prepare beautiful designs for our future.

God's grace had transformed an encounter nine years ago into an amazing providence for today. He turned my sleepless nights into joy and relief. *"The Lord is with me; I will not be afraid. What can man do to me?...I will look in triumph on my enemies. It is better to take refuge in the Lord than to trust in man. It is better to take refuge in the Lord than to trust in princes.... I was pushed back and about to fall, but the Lord helped me" (Psalm 118:6-13).*

If You want it, Take it!

One morning when I picked up the newspaper from our mailbox, an advertisement fell out. At first, I casually glanced at it, but then I was shocked to read its contents. It was an enlargement of the public statement attacking Handong and Young-Gil that had been reported in a local newspaper a few days before. I tried to calm my beating heart. Someone had placed the same ad. in every mailbox of our apartment complex. Pulling out the fliers with shaking hands, I hurried home. *"Then, the fifth time, Sanballat sent his aide to me with the same message, and in his hand was an unsealed letter in which was written… that you and the Jews are plotting to revolt, and therefore you are building the wall. Moreover, according to these reports you are about to become their king" (Nehemiah 6:5-6).*

Before completing the reconstruction of the Jerusalem walls, Nehemiah had to overcome many obstacles. His enemies ridiculed his work, threatened him and plotted against him, and they attempted to block his work by spreading false rumors about him. We experienced the same afflictions that Nehemiah endured. Sometimes we received phone calls in the middle of the night with rough voices that threatened us.

"President Kim! Leave Handong, or be prepared to lose your life!"

Unable to sleep, sometimes we left the phone off the hook for the night. Our adversaries were trying to wear us down. *"They were all trying to frighten us, thinking, 'Their hands will get too weak for the work, and it will not be completed.' But I prayed, 'Now strengthen my hands" (Nehemiah 6:9).*

Not wanting to run into our neighbors, I even avoided going out of the house. Like the Samaritan woman who drew water at the well in the heat of the day in order to avoid people (John 4), I took out the trash late at night. The professor, who lived next-door, encouraged me when she saw my gaunt face.

"I'm actually quite envious of you and President Kim. Not everyone gets to experience such persecution. I too would like to endure that kind of persecution for our Lord! Through all these trials, God will refine the two of you into pure gold," she said.

"Take it all if you're envious! I don't need to become pure gold if it means that I have to go through such frightening harassment," I retorted.

I have Made Your Forehead Harder than Flint

Traveling frequently to Seoul, I tried to keep myself away from people at the airports. One day, I suggested to Young-Gil, "Let's wait in the car for a while longer and go in when they announce the boarding."

The reply that came back was, "Then I will go in first, and you can come in later."

Young-Gil got out of the car and walked into the airport with an easy stride. I could understand how Peter felt when he followed Jesus from a distance. Having his name printed in large letters across newspapers every day did not seem to bother Young-Gil. I asked him, "How can they persecute you like this when our country allows freedom of religion? Even if we were missionaries in a distant country, things wouldn't be this bad. People say that leaders need thick skin, and you certainly must have it. You seem as if everything is okay even though you're in the newspapers everyday."

"How God judges me is more important than how the eyes and ears of men see me," he responded.

"You are not being sent… to many peoples of obscure speech and difficult language, whose words you cannot understand. Surely if I had sent you to them, they would have listened to you. But the house of Israel is not willing to listen to you because they are not willing to listen to me, for the whole house of Israel is hardened and obstinate. But I will make you as unyielding and hardened as they are. I will make your forehead like the hardest stone, harder than flint. Do not be afraid of them or terrified by them, though they are a rebellious house" (Ezekiel 3:5-9).

Was Ezekiel afraid and terrified? God told him to be strong. As I was having my quiet time, I told Young-Gil, "I see now that he has made your forehead like the hardest stone so that you can endure all these frightening trials. Just like Ezekiel!"

His Word for us that day was sweeter than honey, encouraging us so that we can overcome our afflictions. *"Then he said to me, 'Son of man, eat this scroll I am giving you and fill your stomach with it.' So I ate it, and it tasted as sweet as honey in my mouth" (Ezekiel 3:3).*

God Who Lifts Up Our Heads

Beginning in May 1996, banners slandering HGU were posted all over Pohang city. Our attackers even set up tables on busy streets and in front of department stores and lured passersby to sign their petitions. *"O Lord, how many are my foes! How many rise up against me! Many are saying of me, 'God will not deliver him.' ... To the Lord I cry aloud, and he answers me from his holy hill.... Arise, O Lord! Deliver me, O my God!" (Psalm 3:1-7).*

That same year, in the midst of all the attacks, God actually strengthened us. The Ministry of Education declared its intent to reform the university education system, and announced that they would recognize and aid the leading university of innovation and reform. Since Handong had already implemented many innovative educational programs, we felt that this opportunity was designed specifically for Handong.

All summer long, professors prepared the application with the help of many students, while the professors' wives and the students' parents prayed in one heart for Handong to be recognized. When we received the news that Handong had been selected as one of the finalists out of 160 universities in Korea, we were overjoyed. While we all awaited the final announcement, we heard that there were some oppositions, interfering with our final review. Young-Gil and several professors had to prepare additional data and present it to the relevant parties. Our prayers were again filled with tears.

Despite the resistance, Handong was recognized as the most outstanding university for educational reform. A school that had been criticized as a group of religious fanatics was now publicly acknowledged for the quality of its programs just a year after its opening. How ironic it was. Our pain was great, but so was our joy. As if in defense of all the sorrows and persecutions that Handong had endured, we hung a banner at school that read "Handong Global University – Awarded as University of Excellence for Educational Reform." *"You are a shield around me, O Lord; you bestow glory on me and lift up my head" (Psalm 3:3).*

CHAPTER 7:

When a Man Decides To Die

Have You Seen a Corpse Rise?

The school had no money, and a series of nightmarish events occurred one after another like guerrilla attacks. One Sunday morning, barely having washed up, I boarded a plane to Seoul. I wore no make-ups, and my haggard appearance must have made me look like a wounded soldier who had been sent to the rear. I headed to the church. There was still time left before the start of the service, and many people quietly sat reading Bibles throughout the sanctuary. The scene was so serene and peaceful, that it seemed so strange to me. I felt utterly like an outcast.

"I will restore you to health and heal your wounds declares the Lord because you are called an outcast, Zion for whom no one cares" (Jeremiah 30:17). Tears were streaming down my face. I had left on this journey depending on God and following him, but I could no longer walk with my head held high; I felt abandoned. As I sat with my head down and tears in my eyes, the pastor began to preach.

"For the man who has decided to die, success or failure does not matter!"

The opening sentence of his sermon pierced my heart like an arrow. What had been making me so fearful? I realized that it had been the fear of a failure – fear that the school and students would be harmed! Even though I had professed with my mouth that the master of Handong was my God, I had lived as if we had been carrying all the burdens on our own shoulders. We were merely servants, but the servants had been too much caught up with the worries about the work of the master! Once we decided to die, all the conspiracy and violence of our opponents would mean nothing to us, and we would have nothing to fear. Yet, I was bound up with worries and fears because of my awareness of human eyes and ears.

However, the opponents' attacks became increasingly relentless. Finally, blatant criticism of Pastor Ha and Young-Gil were printed in many major newspapers. The statements were printed in four installments, each signed by local notables and organizations. Reports criticizing the school and its president were even delivered to high government officials. How formidable their power seemed! The two accused men were portrayed as immoral leaders of a fly-by-night university. Our hearts were devastated by guilt as we saw Pastor Ha, who had helped the school in times of distress, also defamed because of it. The comfort and courage that I had received from the sermon became only temporary and once again, I was afraid of human eyes and ears.

A voice inside me blamed me, 'You poor soul! You're following Jesus with excessive naïveté. Your husband should have kept working as a KAIST professor and the chairman of the Korea Association for Creation Research, volunteering his time to serve as an elder at a church. How could you fearlessly take responsibility for a school that had lost the financial support, with nothing but faith in God? Do you realize that God is being disgraced because of you? You people have no sense of reality!'

I shook in fear and cried. When Young-Gil saw the newspaper afterward that carried the opponents' articles, he said, "Well, it's not as bad as I thought."

"Not as bad as you thought? How can you say like that? It's great that God have created you with a loose screw in your emotions, giving you dull senses, but I can't stand this because I'm more sensitive than you are. This newspaper will be delivered all over the country, and once people read the articles, what will they think of you and Pastor Ha? This article depicts you and Pastor Ha as immoral people who robbed the school by unethical means! What will happen to your reputation after you lived a clean life as a scientist? And what about Pastor Ha's image as a minister when he had been so well-respected, and...."

Young-Gil calmly interrupted my cry.

"Young-Ae, the Bible verse that you have hung over there on the wall over there, is that for decoration only?" My eyes were drawn to the framed verse.

"I have been crucified with Christ and I no longer live, but Christ lives in me. The life I live in the body, I live by faith in the Son of God, who loved me and gave himself for me" (Galatians 2:20).

After accepting Jesus Christ as my Lord and Savior, this had been my favorite verse, but liking it and living it were not the same. Was God allowing this persecution to teach me to live by this verse not just in my thought but in my life as well? What an agony it is to constantly crucify and erase "me"! Given all the great verses in the Bible, why did I have to be fond of this particular verse? I secretly regretted having liked it, as if the framed verse was the source of all our suffering.

Sometimes, I would stealthily take down the frame from the wall even though the verse had been a reminder of my faith in the past. Then a few days later, I would put it back on its place. The poor guiltless frame experienced turbulence, reflecting my change of mood.

Young-Gil continued, "We have been crucified with Christ, and we are now mere corpses. Have you seen a dead corpse rise up in defense when its name has been defamed? I, Young-Gil Kim, am not such a grand person. My name isn't all that important! A few decades from now, no one will even remember my name. I gave my name to God for his use, but was it only when he lifts up my name, and not when he lowers it? Whether the owner of my name takes my name and stir-fries it or boils it, I have no right to it!"

Finally his peace was passed on to me. I laughed out loud as well and said,

"Well, the name in the newspaper is Young-Gil Kim, not Young-Ae Kim. Since you're fine, I don't care either!"

As I thought about it carefully, I realized that the reason for my despair and temptation was because my ego was too important to me. I was beginning to learn little by little how to be free from all the things that I feared. *"I eagerly expect and hope that I will in no way be ashamed, but will have sufficient courage so that now as always Christ will be exalted in my body, whether by life or by death. For to me, to live is Christ and to die is gain" (Philippians 1:20-21).*

The statement published in the newspapers had great power, but not everyone believed every word in it. Our friends comforted us and said, "God has given you free advertising for Handong Global University! You didn't have to spend a penny! Don't worry. No matter how much Handong and President Kim are attacked in the papers, God will do things beyond our imaginations through all of this. Be thankful that you are under attack. If the school had enough money and was not persecuted in any way, then it would never have become this famous in such a short period of time."

Young-Gil must have been upset himself, but instead he encouraged me.

"We have excellent students, dedicated professors, and furthermore, a great educational program – if we had enough money on top of all that, then we'd have thought that we were leading the school with our own capabilities and end up becoming proud. So consider our lack of funds a blessing."

Young-Gil was an advocate of the Word that awoke my soul. 'Don't avoid their poison-tipped arrows but receive them with your body instead! Be pierced with the arrows of their attacks and kill your old self! My focus is not on them but on you! I will keep My eyes on you until you become crushed and broken through this hellish situation to be molded into tools fit for My use!'

During moments of weakness, my son Ho-Min prayed for me as well.

"God, how is it that you lead us to witness that you are a living God from the very front lines of miracles, in the royal box seats of afflictions, when we are so lacking? We truly thank you, but my mother still misses her father's house in the land of her past, so please touch her heart."

Though the Fig Tree Does not Bud

We have another valuable framed passage on the wall of our house. Our church friends gave it to us as a gift when Young-Gil became an elder in the church.

Giving thanks for the one affliction
Rather than the ten joys that the world gives for free
Fearing the Lord's turning away
More than the ridicule of ten thousand
Becoming the acknowledged servant within the Lord's will
Rather than the man respected according to men's ways
Being the living faith that accomplishes one thing
Rather than the abominable lips that speak a thousand words
Let me become the cornerstone
That glorifies you with Your name and accomplishes Your will

When our friends at church brought us the gift, I said, "I don't like what it says. It says only to thank God for the sufferings He gives us, disowning all worldly happiness. I don't have the confidence to live that kind of a life."

"We picked it thinking that you, being an elder's family, would like it."

"But, the words are too burdensome!"

"Should we exchange it then?"

When I lifted the frame, it felt quite heavy. I could not ask them to exchange it without losing face. I answered, "Well, just leave it. I will try to like it."

I hung it in a dark corner of the living room with an unwilling heart, and I glanced at it once in a while. Even facing it directly was too challenging. I had been shaking with fear ever since arriving at Handong, and one day the framed words came into my heart with clarity. If only I could profess them with faith! *"Though the fig tree does not bud and there are no grapes on the vines, though the olive crop fails and the fields produce no food, though there are no sheep in the pen and no cattle in the stalls, yet I will rejoice in the Lord, I will be joyful in God my Savior"* *(Habakkuk 3:17-18).*

What an awesome profession of faith! But if we were to lose all that we had in reality, our life would be a curse, a life in ruins! Could I still profess that I would be joyful in God? *"The Sovereign Lord is my strength; he makes my feet like the feet of a deer, he enables me to go on the heights" (Habakkuk 3:19).* Could I still declare that I would rejoice because of the joy of salvation and because of my becoming a child of God – even if I seem like a failure in the world's eyes, having lost the reputation, possessions, health, and everything else one by one? Could I live a life of sufficiency whether rich or poor, whether wrongly accused or not, whether in sacrifice or in loss? Even if I could not profess such faith, God's passion and steadfastness would surely lead me to the "heights" where I could give him my declaration – God is my strength!

Encouragers Along the Invisible Path

I met a married couple on the school grounds late one night.

"We come here to Handong on some nights to pray. I once attended the Sunday English worship service at Handong with a foreigner guest. I was deeply moved to see the chapel full of students who understood the English sermon, praising and praying in English. Who can see such a worship service as this anywhere else in Korea? I saw the bright future of hope for Korea.

Whenever I meet local people, I'm disheartened to see how a handful of people with a critical and negative view toward Handong can lead the general opinion. I am saddened to see how President Kim is hated. It is like seeing a feeble young David battling with the giant Goliath. But Mrs. Kim, please don't you worry; only push forward with courage. In the battle with Goliath, David, a man of God won, did he not? There are many spiritual warriors who are praying for Handong and President Kim."

One day, we met Mr. J. Lee, the attorney who had taken charge of the school's defense for free of charge. He was clearly distressed and said,

"Handong's lawsuit is a series of never-ending twists and turns. Sometimes, I've regretted having taken on such a complicated case. If I hadn't volunteered for the work, I probably would have quit long ago. When an attorney does his best for a case, he feels free regardless of the outcome. But Handong's case is different. It is a case that cannot be lost. The future of all the students hangs on the verdict, and all the professors and parents and the Christian community, as well as the countless Handong supporters in and out of Korea, are all watching this case. Above all, God is keeping His eyes on this case, and I feel an incredible pressure. Please pray for me."

His wife commented, "On the first day of Handong's trial in court, another big case that he had taken on won a major victory in the Supreme Court. Since he is working for Handong for free, God has redeemed us through another case."

They said that this was the evidence of God's pleasure that he was serving as Handong's attorney.

One day, a guest visited Young-Gil's office and said,

"I am one of the founders of an organization that has been opposing Handong Global University. It seems to me that a few people and some of the local media are condemning you and Handong one-sidedly, and I came to find out what was really happening."

He was the first person from the local area who wanted to know the truth. Because Handong was being ostracized by the community, whoever openly supported Handong was shunned by them and excluded from the powerful mainstream of the local society. We were grateful for his act of courage. *"Am I now trying to win the approval of men, or of God? Or am I trying to please men? If I were still trying to please men, I would not be a servant of Christ"* *(Galatians 1:10).*

After his visit, we began to notice some changes. He began to arrange meetings between Young-Gil and the local leaders. His actions were prudent and wise. Having been biased by hearing distorted reports about Handong, these leaders slowly began to understand our school. He became the channel of communication between us and the local leaders. (He told us later in retrospect, "President Kim at that time seemed to be up in the air all alone with no one to depend on.")

Anti-Handong Rally and A Miracle

However, attacks against Handong continued without ceasing. The opposition group even held an anti-Handong rally to oppose the school's educational principles. Unaffected by the chaos outside, all was quiet inside the school. The students did not run out to the streets. They did not raise their voices or demand answers as to why these opponents were interfering with their school affairs.

Like King Jehoshaphat and the people of Judah and Jerusalem who bowed to the ground at the temple of the Lord and cried out to God when the men of Moab and Ammon came to attack them, all Handong students knelt and prayed to God. *"Do not be afraid or discouraged because of this vast army. For the battle is not yours, but God's…. You will not have to fight this battle. Take up your positions; stand firm and see the deliverance the Lord will give you" (II Chronicles 15-17).*

A month after the anti-Handong rally, 500 or so Christian leaders from the local area gathered together. Declaring that they could no longer watch accusation against Handong as a group of religious fanatics, they openly and proactively defended us. As a result, our opponents lost some of their momentum. *"The sorrows for the appointed feasts (anti-Handong rally) I will remove from you; they are a burden and a reproach to you. At that time I will deal with all who oppressed you; I will rescue the lame and gather those who have been scattered. I will give them praise and honor in every land where they were put to shame" (Zephaniah 3:18-19).*

Another suffering Young-Gil faced was from the fact that some local people were strongly opposed to the establishment of a genuine Christian university in the city of Pohang. These people insisted that Handong Global University be converted into a public city university instead of keeping it as a private, Christian university. Finally, they initiated a petition drive in the streets and individual houses of Pohang. Those who opposed us obtained approximately 100,000 signatures in support of the conversion of Handong University into a city university. Their argument was that although Handong University was founded in Pohang, the citizens of Pohang did not receive any benefits from it. They argued that since Handong had always attracted students with only outstanding grades in and out of the country, many Pohang area students could not be qualified for admission. They wanted to convert Handong into a school where any student from Pohang area would be admitted without any difficulty. As the president of the university, Young-Gil could not accept the request from the citizens of Pohang, and therefore, he declined. Furthermore, they submitted to the Ministry of Education a 5,000-page petition, with 20 signatures per page, to transform Handong into a public university. The Ministry of Education sent 10 of these pages to Handong as proof that they had received around 100,000 signatories from the local community. The Handong community felt very cornered, as if there were no way out. If the Ministry of Education honored this petition, Handong would face a very difficult challenge indeed. However, again a miracle happened; we discovered that one page of the petition contained a signature stamp of a Handong faculty member. When the school showed that page to this faculty member for verification, he was startled because he had neither seen it before nor signed it! The faculty member whose name was found on that particular page testified that he never signed the petition. Apparently, someone had forged his signature stamp. As a result, we were able to prove that one of the pages that the Ministry of Education had sent to us was actually forged, which discounted the credibility of the entire petition. As the result, the entire signed petition of all 5,000 pages was invalidated by the Ministry of Education. The probability of picking that particular page in a lottery would be one in 5,000. A miracle indeed!! This is just one of the many miracles that God has performed for Handong.

Local people filed numerous lawsuits against Handong and against me. Young-Gil was indicted and had to appear in courts so many times. But God intervened in each one of the lawsuits, and the school won every case.

God Sends the Third Chairman of the Board

Once the emergency passed, Pastor Ha told us of his intent to step down as chairman of the Board. "President Kim, you're under much stress, aren't you? When a tempest comes, we have to let it blow over and wait until it passes. The dark cold winter of Handong will be over, and spring will come soon. When the school was in its worst situation, God gave me the responsibility of being the school's chairman. I will continue to faithfully help and pray for Handong."

Having lost a trusted guardian, we were once again at a loss. However, we could not hold on to Pastor Ha any longer.

We wondered who would readily come onboard this ship of Handong that was being tossed around in the wind and waves and take charge as the captain. But God had prepared yet another man for Handong. It was Dr. Young-Dug Lee, former Prime Minister of the Korean Government who had become the chairman of a Handong sponsoring organization two months before. Those closest to him had advised him not to take on responsibility for a problematic regional university, but Dr. Y. Lee accepted the position of chairman.

"Senior Pastor Ha of Onnuri Presbyterian Church has been attacked for helping Handong, and Handong is still in a dire situation. How can I stay indifferent? God has called an insufficient man like me for a time like this, so I will willingly obey. I am currently the president of the Academy of Korean Studies, but if I were asked to choose between the two, I'd choose Handong in a heartbeat. There are many who can lead the Academy of Korean Studies, but not just anyone can take the post of chairman at Handong right now. I'm fully confident that Handong is God's university with which He is pleased."

One September day in 1996, gusty winds blew across the school grounds where we held the inauguration ceremony for Handong's third chairman. The rough sounds of the wind coming through the loudspeakers were as threatening as the history that Handong had endured so far. Pastor Ha got up on the stage. A thousand emotions passed through me.

"The past 10 months, while I held the post of chairman of the board for Handong, were the most painful and traumatic period in my life, but it was also the most blessed and valuable time of my life. It is because I vividly experienced our God who walks with Handong. Onnuri Church has supported Handong with $8.6 million so far. I realized how our love for God multiplied as we increased our investment in God's work. I believe that no other work is as worthwhile as investing our treasures into training men and women who have God's Kingdom in their hearts. Everyone at the church and I have great love for Handong Global University and our love will not change, but continue because each student at Handong is a precious child of God."

The new chairman, Dr. Y. Lee's inauguration speech followed.

"I think that only the simple-hearted ones have gathered at Handong Global University. President Young-Gil Kim, who gave up a guaranteed life of success and tenure-ship at KAIST, is an odd man indeed, and so are all the professors and the staff members who willingly joined him here. So is the previous Chairman Ha, who underwent great turmoil to save the school from hardship. That is not all. The students who came here when they could have attended prestigious, big-name schools are also strange. However, the parents are even stranger: They devotedly supported their children for 12 years of school education, only to send them to a newly launched university in the countryside.

But all these people have seen a fantastically beautiful world that others cannot see. It is a world that can only be seen through the eyes of faith. I have decided to accept the post of chairman because I too want to be included as one of these odd, simple-hearted people.

Handong is truly a university that I, as a former professor of education at Seoul National University, have dreamed of about all my life. While I served as the Prime Minister of this country, many events occurred in Korea, big and small: A Han River bridge collapsed, a large department store crumbled, and other accidents followed. I once despaired for our country's future. But after visiting Handong, I began to have faith that God has not abandoned us and that our nation has a future.

The educational programs implemented at Handong surprise even an education specialist like me. The policy of 'undeclared major enrollment,' which is the first in Korea, or the system of 'inter-disciplinary education through multiple majors' (in which related fields are tied into a single major) is causing fresh winds of reform among universities in Korea. The students' passion for learning, the professors' love for their students, Handong's emphasis on training its students to become well-rounded persons, the Honor Code, and the social service system: All of these programs add up to education that we cannot see in any other universities. All my lifelong dreams as an education specialist are being realized at Handong. Even more so than when I worked as the Prime Minister, I consider serving you as the chairman of Handong to be a greater honor."

Having turned another corner, Handong with its new Chairman of the Board was now pushing forward through more violent waves.

A Celebration in the Wilderness amid Afflictions

Despite all the difficulties, God allowed us times of celebration. The spring after the school's launch, we wanted to prepare a barbeque for all the students, who had been eating only dormitory food since leaving home. Someone who heard of our intention happily donated the money to purchase the meat. Someone even sent in a donation for barbeque grills.

We bought 400 kilograms of meat to feed our 800 students. The professors' wives excitedly rolled up their sleeves to prepare the food. We divided the meat into 40 portions and marinated it in large plastic bags. The grills, charcoal, and the 40 bags of meat were divided among 40 teams, and the party was to launch as soon as the day's classes ended.

However, the sky began to darken as yellow dust-laden winds blew across campus. We had been very excited about throwing the party just in time for the end of mid-term, and we were very disappointed by the weather. In the afternoon, rain began to fall. Some students played basketball in the rain. It did not look as if the rain would stop anytime soon.

"God, we don't get to celebrate like this very often – please make the rain stop!"

We began to light the charcoal in the drizzling rain. When smoke started rising from the grills here and there, the sky began to break as the wind changed direction, and soon the rain stopped! Everyone beamed. The springs and the autumns of Pohang are often filled with wind, rain, yellow dust and fog, wreaking havoc on airplane schedules. Whenever we had events like this, we prayed with anxious hearts, and then. God always answered us. Some people may say that these are mere coincidences, but I gave thanks to God, because the party in the wilderness could not take place without a particularly good weather in this windy city of Pohang.

Soon the school grounds were filled with the smells of charcoal, smoke, and grilled meat. I felt so happy when I saw Handong students gathered around the grills with chopsticks in their hands, digging in even before the meat was cooked fully. Once they had satisfied their hunger, they leisurely enjoyed each other's company.

There is an old saying, "Nothing feels as good as water entering a dry field and food entering a child's mouth," and I felt truly happy that day. Young-Gil walked and mingled among the students and patted them on their shoulders. The school grounds were filled with the sounds of laughter and singing, and the students were dancing together. All the students, professors, and other Handong family members became one. The party in the wilderness continued late into the night.

Since then, the sweet smell of barbeque on Wednesdays became a part of the Handong tradition.

The Sound of a Ghost ?

There is no corner of Handong that has not been touched by the unseen hands of God, including our basketball court. My son Ho-Min tried to convince me that the school needed a playing surface, saying, "Students can get hurt playing basketball on dirt. Why don't you start fund-raising to build a basketball court, mother? If the school were to do the construction on its own, it shouldn't cost that much."

Knowing the financial situation of the school, the students had not complained that they did not have a basketball court. But how great it would be to have one, and less dangerous for the students when they play!

Some time later, a fund-raising drive began with an earnest heart before God. With the help of a few people, we were able to secure most of the money we needed to build a basketball court. The winter winds were bitter, but my heart was excited by the image of students running around on the new basketball court when winter break was over. A few days before the beginning of the spring semester, one professor stopped a student who was running past her, and asked while pointing to the construction site, "Hey! Do you know what that is?"

"Professor, what is it?"

"It's a basketball court."

The student asked in shock, "Professor, where did we get the money?"

"Where do you think? God gave it to us!"

The student then said, "Now I see! Last night, all the officers of the student government body were working late into early morning. Then, we heard the hissing noise. We got scared and asked among ourselves, 'What is this noise? Are there ghosts?' When we went outside, a man was bending over working on the ground. When we looked at him carefully, it was one of the custodians. I guess he was working on the basketball court!"

The custodian was smoothing the cement ground in the middle of the night. When I heard the story, I had a nice long laugh over the joke about him and the ghost.

King Cyrus of Handong

Ever since the school's opening, Young-Gil emphasized the importance of communal living in dormitories as an integral part of a well-rounded education. "Until now, our country's educational environment has promoted competition, unwittingly pushing students to become selfish rather than considerate and encouraging each other. But at the Handong dormitories, our students, who are different in age, personality, family background, and even nationality and culture, will live together for four years. **"As iron sharpens iron, so one man sharpens another" (Proverbs 27:17).** Our students will refine each other's character and mature as they live together".

I understood Young-Gil's intentions, but the school did not have the fund to build dormitories to accommodate all the incoming students every year. The school was meeting its financial demands with donations and loans. Operating a budget based on unpredictable donations, and building a dormitory on top of that could be considered reckless, which Young-Gil admitted.

"From a management perspective, I'm an "F" student. We have more dormitories than other buildings, which does not make sense. And we build dormitories every year, even with debt!"

However, Young-Gil did not give up his dream of building his students' characters through life education in dormitories. *"You give them something to eat " (Mark 6:37). "He asked this only to test him, for he already had in mind what he was going to do" (John 6:6).* Knowing that His disciples had empty pockets, Jesus gave a command that violated common sense. He wanted to see

His disciples' faith. Knowing our own situation, Jesus seemed to be commanding us, "Build dormitories for the students!" Yet three years after opening the school, we had not yet paid the construction company for their work, and rumors abounded that the school might declare bankruptcy. We wondered if there was a company that would agree to build a dormitory on credit, and we prayed desperately.

"God, please confirm Your will that You want us to build a dormitory. Help us." It did not take long until God gave us a sign that made His will clear. One day Young-Gil said, "The head of a local construction company came to see me today. It is not a large firm, but he said that he would build the dormitory on credit. The dormitory is urgent, but so is the construction of Hyoam Chapel."

The president of the construction company was not a Christian and his company was small. He borrowed the necessary funds by putting his own personal assets as collateral and continued with the construction. After finishing the building, he said to Young-Gil, "I'm not a Christian, but there is something different about Handong and this construction sites. Everyone who works here is always faithful to his or her work. Look at that building. There isn't a brick out of line, and everything has been finished to a tee! And above all else, when I see how the school has gotten to where it is today after having to overcome incredible odds, I feel there must be a God who is certainly watching over Handong. So, I think I'm in danger here: I may become a Christian soon!"

"This is what Cyrus, king of Persia, says: "The Lord, the God of heaven, has given me all the kingdoms of the earth and he has appointed me to build a temple for him at Jerusalem in Judah" *(Ezra 1:2).*

At the dedication ceremony for Hyoam Chapel, Young-Gil delivered a plaque of appreciation to the president and said "We sincerely thank you for completing this beautiful chapel by putting even your personal assets at risk. You are the King Cyrus of Handong."

Our Company Should Finish What We Started!

Women's dormitory was half-built by another construction company when we could not pay a note that became due. The on-site manager of that company came all the way from Seoul to Young-Gil's office with his wife and children.

"President Kim, as the on-site manager, I have to take charge of the construction here. If the school does not pay, then my family has nowhere to go."

A few days later, he said angrily, "We will stop all construction tomorrow and pull out."

"Why all of sudden?"

"We cannot continue the construction when we haven't been paid."

"I understand, but let's talk about it. I'm so sorry that we have not been able to pay you on time." Young-Gil asked.

He pretended not to hear and left the room without looking back. A few days after this outburst, he came back to the office with a big smile on his face.

"My company decided to finish the dormitory construction."

"What happened?"

"We should finish what we started! A few days ago, we had a meeting with all the on-site managers around the country. During the meeting, I insisted that we must complete the construction at Handong. I said that the students at Handong are different from students of other schools. They never pass by the construction site without saying hello and thanking us for our work. Other than the fact that it has no money, Handong is truly a great university. Fortunately, the company decided to support me. Once we're finished building the dormitory, what is the company going to do even if you don't pay? Pull down the building?"

As construction neared its end, the on-site manager came to school with $1,700. He and his workers had saved money by spending less on food and snacks, so that they could donate it as a scholarship fund for Handong. Later on, he was truly aware of the school's difficulties, and helped the school in many ways. He had been studying for a technical license exam while working on the Handong construction project, and we were overjoyed when we heard that he passed it with flying colors and was promoted in his company.

Finally, the beautiful women's dormitory was completed. The students moved into the dorms while the construction bills were still pending. The new women's dormitory was fancier in design than the others, and the envious male students called it a "hotel."

Crisis in the Desert

Toward the end of 1997, when many countries in Asia, including Korea, experienced financial crisis, the school's financial situation worsened. We could hardly breathe under the pressure, and we had barely enough money to cover our daily expenses. Eventually, we could not pay wages to our professors and staff. The company, which had built the beautiful women's dormitory, had cooperated with us as much as possible, but we could no longer delay our payment. Then, the bank that had agreed to give us a line of credit called with an unexpected news.

"We're sorry, but a very important customer of ours has threatened not to bank with us unless we sever all relations with Handong. We do not have any alternative."

Unseen hands of opposition had relentlessly been working ceaselessly against us. Taking advantage of the moment, Satan whispered in my ear, "If the school declares bankruptcy, then government-appointed trustees will sit on your board, and the school will become a non-Christian school in accordance with their demands. Young-Gil may end up in court, and you may be shamed before the world. You've already received countless indictments and have ended up in court multiple times."

As I was reciting the "what-if" scenario in my head, Young-Gil was poring over Nehemiah like a shipwrecked man looking at his compass.

Even though Young-Gil and I had seen the workings of the living God at Handong countless times, we continuously needed to reconfirm God's faithfulness and ability to intervene, whenever situations sprung up that could not be resolved by man. We had no source of money, and when promissory notes worth $1 million or $2 million became due, we despaired to the point of wanting to give up. The interest on our loans kept ballooning. Sometimes, we needed to borrow a few thousand dollars just to cover operating expenses.

Only those who have borrowed money would know how desperate we felt. Living in debt meant not merely a loss of pride but also scorn and disdain. Before becoming the president of Handong, Young-Gil had seldom been to a bank! He had hardly been aware of how much money was in his wallet. Perhaps, that was why he was able to say so easily that he needed a few hundred thousand dollars.

Must harsh trials and tribulations follow when we try to apply God's word to our life? No matter where we looked, there were no sources of money for the school. We were passing through a frightening desert of destitution. That Sunday, Pastor Ha gave a sermon on the Israelites' wanderings through the desert.

"The desert requires us to look only upon the Word of God. The desert is a place where we realize our absolute incompetence, but the true crisis of the desert is not a lack of food or water. The most dangerous crisis is when we begin to doubt whether God truly lives."

I recounted once more how God had faithfully guided my life until now. *"My eyes are fixed on you, O Sovereign Lord; in you I take refuge – do not give me over to death. Keep me from the snares they have laid for me, from the traps set by evildoers. Let the wicked fall into their own nets, while I pass by in safety" (Psalm 141:8-10).*

Whether it be a dormitory, the chapel or an engineering building each of every buildings in Handong Campus is stained with tears that carry silent testimonies as to how God used the building when it was constructed - to show that He is in control and He is indeed the helping God. Truly, He is the living God who does not let cries of His believers pass without His intervention. This was His way to show the world, that Handong is His school that He founded for his Great Commission.

CHAPTER 8:

Moses in a Papyrus Basket

The Birth of the Papyrus Basket

At the time of Moses' birth in the Old Testament, all the Hebrew male babies born in Egypt were ordered to be killed. Moses' fate was like a candle in a storm.

"We can no longer raise this child in hiding. We must now send him down the river, entrusting his life to God's hands," Moses' parents made a bold decision.

They must have mourned and wailed as they weaved the papyrus basket in which they would lay their baby. But God moves human hearts, and He miraculously saved the life of Moses through the hands of an Egyptian princess, the very daughter of the king who attempted to kill all Hebrew male babies. The papyrus basket thus played a crucial role in rescuing Moses, who later became the leader of the Israelites. *"She became pregnant and gave birth to a son. When she saw that he was a fine child, she hid him for three months. But when she could hide him no longer, she got a papyrus basket for him and coated it with tar and pitch. Then she placed the child in it and put it among the reeds along the bank of the Nile. His sister stood at a distance to see what would happen to him" (Exodus 2:2-4).*

The school had undergone wrenching birth pains and frightening persecutions that had exceeded our imagination. No longer were able to hide our poverty amidst the escalating financial crisis, we decided to weave a basket as well. A professor from KAIST suggested that we begin a fund-raising drive of '$1 or $10 per account' in which anyone could participate. A few professors named the fund-raising drive the "Papyrus Basket." Each strand of papyrus was weak, yet countless strands came together to form the basket that saved Moses' life. Likewise, a donation of $1 or $10 was like a single strand of papyrus. However, the Papyrus Basket woven with the prayers of our supporters would become the tar and pitch that protect Handong against secularization.

As the Papyrus Basket housed Moses who was later used as a God's man to save the world's race, Handong Global University is the Papyrus Basket that housed God's children who will grow to be used by God to save all nations. The Papyrus Basket contained our desperate faith, that Handong is God's school and He is on our side and guides us for protection.

In February of 1998, not long after the Papyrus Basket was launched in Korea,, the Handong International Foundation (HIF) was born at the Cornerstone Church located in 24428 S. Vermont Ave., Harbor City, California 90710 as a nonprofit tax-exempt organization. (E-mail:lahandong@hotmail.com) Tel. (310) 530-4040

Shortly afterwards, HIF chapters were established in Washington, D.C. and Seattle, Washington. Whenever an HIF chapter was launched, Young-Gil said, "In the twenty-first century, we must endow our young men and women with the purpose of learning the value and meaning of life. Our country does not have many natural resources, but God blessed us with an abundance of able people. Thus, the future of our country depends on our educational system. There is an old Chinese saying, 'Looking ahead one year, plant wheat. Looking ahead 10 years, plant trees. But for the vision and dreams of 100 years, raise people.' The most worthwhile investment for our future is to cultivate leaders. You too can support Handong, where we can raise honest and competent leaders who worship and fear God. It is certainly a good opportunity as well as a privilege for any one to help to raise God's people."

In Washington, D.C., we held several Handong support gatherings. At a fund-raising event in 1998 before the Korean community, the leading pastor said, "We all have our own alma maters, but we need to support Handong because it is God's university. There are several reasons why we call Handong a university of God.

"First, Handong's educational principle is based on the faith of God the Creator. Today, it is difficult for our children to have true faith because they are taught in schools that evolution is viewed as the truth. Second, just as Jesus Christ trained His disciples while He was here on earth, the professors of Handong are raising up their students to become disciples of Jesus by teaching them God's Word and faith in addition to professional knowledge. Third, Handong has no human owner. The owner of Handong is God. Supporting Handong in producing leaders who worship our God is God's work as well as the true act of patriotism.

Pastor John Harvard came to the United States from Great Britain, and when he passed away in 1637, he gave his entire life-savings of $1,254 and 320 books to a small university that had been founded a year earlier. Built on such a foundation, the university was called Harvard, and today Harvard produces many fine scholars and national leaders and is still producing them. When I visited Handong after only hearing about it, I came away with the hope that Handong will produce the miracle of raising Moses-like leaders of our people who will change the twenty-first century world. If all of us gather our strength in support of Handong, then great Christian professionals, who will lead our times in each of their fields of expertise, will march out of Handong."

In the summer of 1999, at a Handong support gathering in Washington, D.C., one Korean politician, who happened to be visiting the city, delivered a congratulatory remark.

"Korea ranks No. 3 in the world in terms of population density. If dishonesty and makeshift laws were rampant, our country would be like hell. On the other hand, if the country were to have the reputation of honesty in the global community, our powers would propel us upward with an explosive force. Many universities pride themselves on their outstanding educational program, but not many schools train their students in accordance with God's curriculum to practice honesty by conducting non-proctored exams for example. Handong Global University emphasizes the whole person education that trains student's intellect, spirit, and character, and I am certain that Handong will bring honor to Korea on the international stage. When I visited Handong after only hearing about it, I came away with the hope that Handong will produce the miracle of raising Moses-like leaders of our people who will change the twenty-first century world. If all of us gather our strength in support of Handong, then great Christian professionals, who will lead our times in each of their fields of expertise, will march out of Handong."

Just as God watched over Moses housed inside the papyrus basket, Handong's papyrus basket, woven by our caring supporters and containing the future leaders of our time, is growing not only within Korea but in the United States and in the world as well.

I'm Rejoicing Night and Day

My testimony ministry began by chance. One day in November 1996, Senior Pastor Han-Eum Oak of Sarang (Love) Community Church in Seoul asked Young-Gil to give a testimony at his church. However, we realized that Young-Gil had mistakenly booked two commitments on the same evening. When we told Pastor Oak about it, he suggested that I speak on my husband's behalf. I headed toward Sarang Community Church in Seoul with a heart that was beating rapidly. As I entered the sanctuary, the hymn that the congregation was singing moved my heart.

> Oh faithful Lord, oh faithful Lord
> I will never leave you.
> I will never forsake you.
> Our Lord promised us
> And He keeps His promise.
> He will protect me from now
> Forever more.

Like a small girl who had endured rough treatment outside and was now sitting in her father's strong arms, recounting her sorrows, I cried over and over before I stood in front of the congregation. That was the start of my testimonial ministry. Whenever I go to an assembly as a guest speaker, I tuck the Papyrus Basket pamphlets into my bag. Sometimes I muster up the courage to talk about it, but sometimes I could not bring up the subject myself to mention it.

"Handong Global University has no human lords but God as its Lord. It is a university largely run with the support of Christians. It is a university that churches must help."

Of the countless churches to which I had been invited, a few stand out in my memory. When I visited a church nearby Seoul in 1999, I cautiously mentioned the Papyrus Basket. The pastor, however, readily replied, "I'd actually been wondering how we could help Handong. Thank you for giving me the opportunity today. Handong is the pride of Korean Christianity."

After I finished my testimony, he went up on the stage and said, "Participating in God's work is the rightful duty of us believers. It is a work that pleases our Lord. I hope that every one of you will join the efforts to help Handong Global University today."

He himself filled in his supporter's form on the stage before the congregation, and I could soon see others following him. After the service, he gave me two large envelopes. When I came home, Young-Gil and one of the professors, who had been to another church that evening, were waiting for me with big smiles.

"Mrs. Kim, we added many supporters to the Papyrus Basket today."

I took out my envelopes as well. "I did too. Look!"

I felt refreshed as I saw their joyful faces.

I'm rejoicing night and day
As I walk the pilgrim way
For the hand of God in all my life I see
And the reason of my bliss
Yes, the secret of all is this
That the Comforter abides with me
He abides, He abides
Hallelujah, He abides with me!
I'm rejoicing night and day
As I walk the narrow way
For the comforter abides with me
(H. Buffum, 1879-1939)

It is not Yours but Mine

One afternoon, I received a letter from a stranger. Looking outside into the darkness through a frosted window, I re-read the letter attentively. No matter how dark it was outside, there was a bright light in my heart. The letter read,

"The day you visited my church, I offered a truly moving worship to our God. I was so thankful that there is a Christian school with a vision such as Handong's! I know that the result of a righteous battle will surely be a victory. I believe that our Lord has crowns prepared for you and President Kim, who are bearing the pains of our Lord.

I love God with all my heart, and I want to live for God. I had been walking a life of faith with confidence as I managed my business, making much money and giving large offerings. But pride began to sprout in my heart, and I began to compromise with the world when it came to making money. I began to rationalize my actions. I pretended to be holy when I was at church, but I had turned into a disappointment in God's eyes.

In the meantime, my company had to declare bankruptcy after a massive accident. From then on, hardships fell upon my family. No matter what new business I attempted, I ended up having to fold in less than a year. I cried out to God.

'Oh God, did I not pray that I would support your work? I'm not trying to run a business just to satisfy my own stomach, so why do you let it fail so miserably?'

My apartment was auctioned off, and my family had no place to go. We moved to a cheap rental with $5,000 as security and $350 rent per month. We could not fall any lower than where we were. As we were unable to pay for electricity, I lit a candle and my young daughter asked whose birthday it was, and started singing 'Happy Birthday.' When we ran out of rice, my wise wife would cheerfully say that she felt like eating noodle for breakfast and ate it with the children. But even then, I believed that God would never abandon me.

Later on, God granted me another opportunity to start a business, and he began to restore my life bit by bit. The day you came to our church, I had collected my first payment of $10,000 and ran to make to the service on time with the check still in my wallet. My heart was beating just thinking about how excited my wife would be when I gave her this check. But as I was listening to your testimony, God kept telling me to donate all the money to Handong.

'Did you not pray that you would run your business for missions and scholarships? Haven't you been unable to give any offerings for the past few years as your businesses have failed? And isn't that money not yours, but in fact, mine?'

Without hesitation, I said 'amen' and participated in supporting Handong.

God comforted me that day and said, 'My son, your entire net worth is your rent security of $5,000, but since you gave me $10,000, you have given me twice as much as all your possessions.'

I was overjoyed that day. Mrs. Kim, aren't you curious about how God has blessed me since then?

God gave me overflowing work, and I was able to purchase a factory for $800,000. Two years after starting my business, I now have about 40 employees with a 71,000 square-feet plant. God has been leading me in amazing ways through my second factory purchase, which is now underway.

Mrs. Kim, thank you for giving me the opportunity to be led by God. I desire to live my life loving nothing else but God and holding nothing else more valuable than God. I too pray for Handong and President Kim. I hope to visit Handong someday. Hallelujah!"

Unforgettable Memories

One day, as I wrapped up my testimony at a church and was leaving the stage, the pastor grabbed my hands.

"Mrs. Kim, God does not accept sacrificial offering from just anyone. I am confident that God will turn Handong's affliction into a great victory."

He said to each elder coming into the pastor's office, "Our church must help Handong Global University."

It was as if he was getting each person to give his promise. Two days later, the pastor called me.

"Mrs. Kim, our church has decided to support Handong with $50,000."

The donation exactly matched the cost of our taxes and fees that month.

One day in March 2000, as I was getting off an airplane in Busan, I took a wrong step on the stairs and fell forward. I twisted my foot and it started swelling up. The next day, I left the house limping to go to Jeonju city. I placed my foot on top of the heater in the bus thinking that it might help reduce the swelling, but my foot continued to swell. After I finished speaking, the people who had invited me dropped me off at Jeonju terminal station. I was rather disappointed.

'Couldn't they at least take me to Daejon train station, an-hour drive from here, where it's more convenient for me to go home? How could they leave me here like this?'

Ignoring a beggar whom I saw in the corner of my eye, I struggled to climb up the stairs, dragging my feet. Then, I heard a voice in my heart.

"If I were standing there, would you ignore me?"

I climbed back down the stairs, and politely put some money in his hands. I regretted having to climb the stairs twice because of my inconsiderate action the first time.

After missing my bus by a few seconds, I was dismayed to learn that I would have to wait a long time for the next bus with my foot in pain. I was mad at the clerk.

"I missed my bus because you didn't give me the right gate number!"

I did not realize that I had raised my voice. It was even more painful to see how I was behaving. I had to wait another three hours for the next bus. When Young-Gil called me on my cellular phone, I replied bluntly. In the waiting area, an old lady sitting next to me started speaking to me, "Excuse me, where can I find the bus that goes to Seoul?"

"Go to the second gate over there," I answered.

She asked again and again.

I was irritated. "I already told you the gate number several times. There is still plenty of time before your departure, so I'll tell you again when time comes." A woman who was sitting on my left leaned forward and said to the old lady in a friendly voice, "I'm also going to Seoul, so you can follow me."

Again, I felt like a failure. God seemed to be showing me a model through the kindness of the woman on my left, and ask, "Why are you so grouchy today?"

What can be done about this wicked nature in me that refuses to be broken! Lord, please take pity on me! *"Be imitators of God, therefore, as dearly loved children and live a life of love, just as Christ loved us and gave himself up for us as a fragrant offering and sacrifice to God" (Ephesians 5:1-2).*

As soon as I sat in the bus, I placed my foot on the hot heater again. (I only learned later that a swollen foot needs ice packs instead of heat since heat actually worsens the swelling.) Then, I realized that I needed to pray for my foot.

"God, people say that acupuncture is good for situations like this, but there is no time for it. Please heal it with your hands."

All the fatigue that had been accumulating since early morning rushed over me, and I fell asleep in my seat. When I walked into our house late at night, Young-Gil wanted to see my foot. At that moment, I was amazed. I forgot that I had a pain on my foot until that time. My foot did not hurt even though I tried poking it with my fingers, and the swelling had completely gone without even a bruise. *"I am the Lord who heals you" (Exodus 15:26).*

God was with me whenever I spoke at a rally. He added many people to pray for Handong and supporting it financially.

The Papyrus Basket, the Shield for Handong

As of September 2005, the Papyrus Basket has over 20,000 members and 1,600 churches throughout Korea and abroad who advocate Handong. Many graduates have sent their first month's salaries to Alma Mater Handong. It is a Korean tradition for young men and women to offer their first month's salaries of their first jobs to their parents as an expression of thanks and respect. The Papyrus Basket is the lifeline of Handong. The prayers and financial support of the countless family members of the Papyrus Basket has been a shield against rough times and violent storms for the debt-ridden frail institution of Handong with uncertain future.

We are earnestly praying for the Papyrus Basket membership to increase to 50,000 for our special global educational activities to fulfill our Lord's Great Commission through the Papyrus Basket.

One of Korea's major newspapers, *Joong-Ang Daily* wrote an article titled "Graduation News – Generous Donation of First Month's Salaries to their Alma Mater." The article reported that many graduates of Handong, which was about to celebrate its sixth graduation, continued to demonstrate their love for their Alma Mater by donating not only their first month's salaries but also a pledge of a fixed amount per month afterwards as well. Some graduates were quoted as saying that their love for the school grew even bigger after graduation and that they planned to continue to help the school into the future.

The Bible records countless names throughout its pages – some of which we find difficult to pronounce. Some joyfully participated in God's work and sacrificed their possessions for the temple in Jerusalem, for the tabernacle in the desert, for the sanctuary, and for Nehemiah's rebuilding of the Jerusalem walls (Nehemiah 3, 7). *"Bezalel, Oholiab and every skilled person to whom the Lord has given skill and ability to know how to carry out all the work of constructing the sanctuary are to do the work just as the Lord has commanded" (Exodus 36:1).*

I have no doubt that God considers precious all those who participate in God's work. *"If anyone gives even a cup of cold water to one of these little ones because he is my disciple, I tell you the truth, he will certainly not lose his reward" (Matthew 10:42).*

The Boaz Plan

While supporters of the Papyrus Basket provided for the immediate financial needs of Handong, we also launched the Handong Boaz Family Plan in 2001. Through it, we planned to pay back Handong's loans and create a springboard so that the school can leap forward and become internationalized. There is a story behind this Boaz plan:

One day, I was introduced to Ms. C. Suh, a businesswoman.

She said, "For several years, I've experienced firsthand the difficulties of fund shortages while managing my own company, so I know what that feels like better than anyone. When I read about President Kim's imprisonment, I could not sleep that night. Managing a school's affairs as president is already a huge challenge! I was also worried that some people might have a wrong impression of President Kim. I felt relieved when I heard that most people were aware that President Kim was in the current situation because of the financial difficulties of the school.

"Mrs. Kim, I too have received a lot of training regarding money. Now, God has opened the doors of blessing rather than difficulties, and my company is doing pretty well. God is leading, and I'm just following. Reflecting on my days when I suffered because of lack of money, I wanted to encourage President Kim. Recently, I'd been thinking of closing my business, but because of Handong, I've discovered a new reason to continue to work hard. It's not much, but I'd like to help Handong."

She handled me an envelope. A short while later, when she made her second donation, she said: "Mrs. Kim, God has given me a thought in preparing the $10 million that Handong needs. Handong's difficult financial situation and Handong's good image have become widely known. There are many people who want to help the school but don't know what concrete steps to take, so why don't we look for 10,000 people who love Handong. If each of them donates $1,000, then we will have $10 million. I've shared my thoughts with a few others, and they said they would be glad to help." Encouraged by her words, we began our Handong Boaz Family Plan.

As a witness of Handong's living history, I cannot but think that the whole scenario of Handong is nothing but God's plan being realized right in front of us.

Chapter 9:

God Who Fills Our Cup

As He fed Elijah in the Desert

"Handong Global University is God's university where God's people are trained in God's ways!" What a grand title! What a rigorous training we had to endure as we learned God's ways. It seemed as if He was determined to teach us that the basics of faith go well beyond the bounds of reality.

At the end of 1997, Korea underwent a national economic crisis when the nation's reserves of foreign currencies depleted. Many companies collapsed and the government launched a campaign to collect U.S. dollars and gold. The school finance was in extreme difficulties as well, but there was no reduction in the number of supporters for the Papyrus Basket – the lifeline of Handong. Many people who were concerned about the school asked, "Things at school must be tough these days, aren't they?"

I replied, "Our school was in an economic crisis since the day we opened any way, so we feel relatively less poor now that things are difficult for everyone."

At that time, a businessman in Los Angeles donated $1 million, asking that his name remain anonymous. Insisting that he was merely running an errand for God to take the money that God had given him and send it to God's university, he thanked God for allowing him to do this work. Many Koreans living in the United States sent generous donation and scholarship funds.

However, the school's financial situation continuously worsened. Finally, one day Young-Gil came home and told me that he could not pay some of faculty staff salaries. My heart sank. I ran to the bathroom, turned on the shower and sat under the streams of water with my clothes on and cried. Young-Gil said to me calmly, "God knows all our needs, and God's providence must be at work here."

Even though I knew that Satan was playing with my heart, I could not but listen to the voice that asked, "Aren't you being too simple-minded in your faith?" Late that evening, a basket of red carnations was delivered to our house. Among the flowers was a carefully written card.

"We had not realized that the school was in such a difficult financial situation. President Kim, how painful it must have been for you to bear such a heavy burden all on your own. We are walking with you, so take courage!"

It was from some professors. Their wives also encouraged me.

"Mrs. Kim, we are Handong's family, too. Nothing will happen to us even if our salaries are delayed, so please don't worry."

Some professors opened lines of credit from their banks to help with the school's operating expenses, and some moved to the school's guesthouses so that their rent deposits could be added to the school funds. These emergency measures helped the school avoid a few desperate crises for the moment.

The professors said, "Missionaries don't receive salaries, do they? This is a chance for us to experience how God used the ravens to feed Elijah!"

Regardless of the professors' stand, Young-Gil was soon indicted with charges of misfeasance and misappropriation of funds for illegally borrowing the professors' rent deposits. The professors were summoned one by one to testify as to whether the President had covertly pressured and extorted them. They replied: "We were aware of the school's financial situation, and we would have contributed more if we could. Even those who do not have any relation with Handong support our school. What we have done is nothing."

Some professors used pay phones for personal calls in order to save the school's phone bills, and all the staff and students tried to save even a single sheet of paper, a drop of water, and a light bulb. Several parents started a campaign to pay tuition in advance. *"Carry each other's burdens, and in this way you will fulfill the law of Christ" (Galatians 6:2).*

Tell God Directly

"It is a blessing that Handong does not have money," Young-Gil told me. "We have wonderful professors, excellent students, and a great educational program, so would we have really depended on God if we did not have any financial worries?"

"How can not having enough fund to run the school be a blessing? The school doesn't have any money because you keep saying it's a blessing that we don't have any. Don't say things like that anymore," I retorted.

However, one day Young-Gil, who is always optimistic, became discouraged. He tried to recruit financial support all day long but to no avail. We had received several late notices on our taxes and fees, and our electricity was to be cut off if we did not pay that day. We had already taken out a loan with our house as security and obtained financing through our personal savings accounts.

"We must have $20,000 today. It's an even bigger miracle that the school is this poor!"

He laughed out of despondence. I heard his desperate prayers from his study. Sometime later, when I looked inside the quiet room, he was lying huddled on the floor. My heart cringed. He too was in despair.

"Young-Gil, God knows all our urgent needs, and He must have prepared something that we do not know about yet. We have never failed before because of a lack of money. God is the Lord of this university, and the one who is Lord must care about the situation even more than we do."

This time, it was I who was comforting my husband. I started to call on God.

"God! Give us some money. Look at him. Doesn't Your heart ache too, watching him lying like that with no more strength? Send us some money that will make him jump up from the floor!"

I kept hassling God. At 2 pm, the phone rang. I ran to answer it.

"This is the house of Handong's President, right? I am a pastor's wife at a church in Incheon city. I want to send a donation to Handong, so please let me know the bank account number. For several days now, the Holy Spirit has been pressing me to send money to Handong, saying that it's in desperate situation. We opened a certificate of deposit as an offering for North Korean missions, but I will send it to Handong today."

I was overjoyed, but without knowing what I was saying, I heard strange words coming out of my mouth.

"How can you give a missionary offering to us?"

"If I don't obey, then God will rebuke me," she answered.

I then confessed, "God has told you of our situation! Our circumstances are actually very urgent right now."

I ran to the study.

"Young-Gil, get up! God has seen you lying down like this. Someone is sending $10,000 to the school right now!"

The phone rang again. It was a message that an attorney who had just opened his office had decided to send his first retainer of $3,500 to the Papyrus Basket.

"I'd like to know his name," I said.

"He didn't want his name revealed. He said that it is enough that God knows." The speaker on the other side of the line replied.

Soon the wire transfer from the Incheon pastor was posted, and the rest of the needed funds filled the Papyrus Basket as well. Seeing the breathtaking events of the day, we experienced first-hand the God of George Mueller, whom we had only read about before. We felt the breath of God, who intervenes at critical moments and never leaves us on our own. When Jesus appeared to the grief-stricken disciples, Peter recognized Jesus first and ran to Him, crying out "It is He!" And just like Peter, we too cried out, "Wow! He truly lives!"

When a child who is learning to walk opens his arms for help, what father would not readily hold his hands? We realized that God worked when we became completely helpless. God's love was bigger than our needs.

Lord, we Need $5 Million!

In July 1998, after speaking at the Korean Students Abroad (KOSTA) at Wheaton College in Chicago, we worshipped at a Korean-American church in Washington, D.C. on Sunday. The pastor's sermon that day was on the blind man, Bartimaeus. During his message, he suggested to the congregation, "Everyone has an earnest prayer topic. Let us pray for a few seconds like Bartimaeus who cried out, 'Son of David, Jesus, have mercy on us.'"

We all bowed down our heads in a short prayer. I whispered to Young-Gil, who was sitting next to me, "What did you pray for?"

"I prayed God to send $5 million to our school!"

As always, he was filled with worries about the school's finances. After the benediction, the pastor said, "If anyone has an illness or a desperate prayer, come up to the stage and I will pray for you."

Young-Gil ran up to the stage before the pastor had even finished uttering his last word and knelt in front of the pastor. It happened almost instantly. Like Bartimaeus, he cared less as to how he would appear to others in the congregation that we were visiting for the first time.

Toward the end of that year, on an afternoon with a dark sky heavy with snow clouds, we received an unexpected phone call. A businessman we had known for a long time had decided to donate $5.8 million to Handong. $5.8 million! For a moment, we thought we were dreaming. I called the school.

"Hello, Vice President Oh? Someone just wired a $5.8 million donation to the school. Hello? Hello?"

There was a dead silence on the other end. A few minutes later, I heard, "Yes, I just received notice from the bank as well. I can't believe such a thing has happened to us."

Mr. Oh, who had been promoted to vice president of HGU to take charge of the school's finance, could not continue. It had been five months since Young-Gil's desperate Bartimaeus prayer. *"I will give you the treasures of darkness, riches stored in secret places, so that you may know that I am the Lord, the God of Israel, who summons you by name" (Isaiah 45:3).*

Later, the school treasurer said, "Without that donation, all the school's operations would have come to a halt. Where do we begin to pay off our urgent debts? The school has so many notes that it will take several days just to sort everything out. I'm so amazed by the fact that the school now has money that I don't want this day to end."

Young-Gil and I prayed, "Our Lord who exceeds all our imaginations, we thank You for this wonderful gift. Please remember the donator and bless him. We pray in the name of Jesus, who led us to pray five months ago for this blessing that You have given us today. Amen."

Even now, whenever I think about that day, I cry out in astonishment. I experienced our God who is boundless and mighty. *"Until now you have not asked for anything in my name. Ask and you will receive, and your joy will be complete" (John 16:24).*

Answer to a Prayer of 50 Years

One day in May 1999, I met a kind-looking woman pastor, from Los Angeles, who was then 75 years old. She came who came to see us at Handong. She held my hands and said,

"Mrs. Kim, as I listened to your testimony on tape, I was reminded of myself 40 years ago and I cried a lot. I can understand your labors and tears better than anyone else. Fifty years ago, when my uncle and my husband founded a university in Seoul and were managing the school, I prayed with tears and heartache in the background. In 1968, when my husband passed away suddenly, I immigrated to the United States with five children. Though living thousands of miles away, I continued to pray that a university would be founded on a pure Christian faith based on pure Christian faith in my home country. I believe that Handong is the answer to my prayers of 50 years. I came to visit to offer my small encouragement to everyone at Handong who is working so wholeheartedly."

On that day, while late spring rain was falling, she gave us a yellowed land deed that she had kept for 40 years. She donated 46,300 square feet of land near Seoul to Handong.

"President Kim, this is only a small gift, but please accept it since it is the entire possession of a widow. These are my last two coins here on earth that I give to my Lord who loves me."

She had come with the paperwork necessary for the transfer of the property prepared by the Korean consulate general in Los

Angeles and government offices in Seoul. In less than two hours, the transfer was complete.

"If I had a last wish, it would be for Handong to produce many men and women of faith who will lead our country."

Coincidentally, on the day of her visit, Young-Gil had been explaining the school's difficult situation to the professors, as we had been unable to pay their salaries for three months. She was in the room at the time, and she said,

"Beloved professors! Is Jesus Christ truly your God? If you believe that Jesus Christ is the living God and the Lord who died for us, then there couldn't be any loss or sacrifice too big for us to give to Him. If we truly believe in Him, then how could we complain? How can it be the responsibility of the President that you have not received your salaries? Handong does not belong to either President Kim or Chairman Lee.

"You are in the most blessed positions right now since God is training you here. This is the time when we can experience the living God, first-hand. To each of the professors here today – look unto your God. My church is a small church, but the entire congregation has been praying for Handong for a long time. Do not lose courage. Do not lose heart. Our God lives!"

Should We Place an Advertisement, too?

"Young-Ae, come and read this book. It's the same story as our school. If you change the title, it would be Handong's story," Young-Gil said one day as he read *The Story of Keochang Christian High School*. He laughed out loud.

Fifty years ago, during the early days Keochang Christian High School's establishment, the school underwent an extremely difficult financial situation. Their stories of debts and lawsuits sounded so similar ours.

When Mr. Y. Chun completed his studies in the United States and took on the post of principal at the school, all the students had withdrawn except for eight. He cut the teachers' salaries in half and tried diligently to salvage the school, but the financial difficulties worsened. As the debt ballooned, the school faced seizure if it did not pay off the money and interest in time. Not knowing what to do, Mr. Chun decided to fast for a week and went up to a mountain.

After four days of prayer, he sat on a rock, full of resentment toward God who provided no answers, and said, "God, did I come here wanting to make money? Or did I come for here for an honor? I came here because You sent me here to spread the Gospel. If I pack and leave because I am not able to pay off the debt, then who'd be more shamed? So, You should think about this situation twice! I'll pay to place an advertisement in the newspapers that will read 'God doesn't exist,' to warn people not to suffer losses by being deceived by You even if I have to sell my tiny rice paddy back home to pay for the advertisement!"

Suddenly he looked at the deep valleys, the beautiful mountainsides, the colorful trees, and the evening sunset. The better a machine is made, the more silently it runs, he realized. The sun rises and evening comes without fail. The four seasons arrive every year, and the earth continuously turns on its axis in an orbit – could the logic and harmony of it all exist without God the Creator? How could a masterpiece exist without a painter? Unconsciously, he began to praise out loud.

This is my Father's world
And to my listening ears
All nature sings, and round me rings
The music of the spheres
This is my Father's world
I rest me in the thought
Of rocks and trees, of skies and seas
His hand the wonders wrought
(M. D. Babcock, 1901)

He bowed down his head and said, "God, I repent. I take back the words I spoke a moment ago. I doubted Your existence and Your love for a brief moment. Whether You take care of the debt or not, I will continue to work diligently at the Keochang High School."

When he returned to the school a few days later, a wire message was waiting for him.

"$2,050 has been posted to your bank account."

It was from a friend from his seminary in the United States.

Young-Gil especially liked this passage. Whenever the school's finances got difficult, he would say, "God, should we place an advertisement, too?"

False Refuge

The school's financial problems continued without resolution, and lawsuits hit us one after another. I felt as if we were going to suffocate.

"God, if things are this difficult, we will collapse from exhaustion."

Then, one day, Young-Gil said, "Young-Ae, I'm going to submit my formal resignation to KAIST and use my severance pay to pay the staff's salary."

My heart sank. Young-Gil had taken a leave of absence from KAIST to take his post at Handong. His severance pay, accumulated over 17 years, was our secret safety net that we had stashed away for our retirement. Whenever we felt worn down, I had taken comfort in knowing that at least we could still go back to KAIST. But now, my husband wanted to completely part ways with everything safe.

Once, when we were driving down the highway to Seoul from Pohang, I stared in the distance at the KAIST Science Park in the distance that we passed by in our trip, until it disappeared out of my sight. "Our days when we were living there were so carefree!"

One day, when Young-Gil came back from a visit to KAIST, I asked him, "How are things there? Is everyone fine?"

He answered plainly, "Yes, it's still a peaceful place."

"Don't you miss our days there?" I asked.

Knowing where I was headed, he said, "What are you trying to tell me? God knows all your inner thoughts in your mind. Don't ever say things like that."

I could not say a word. This time as well, I could only say, "I'll pray about it." It was an excuse. Wanting to fend off Young-Gil for the moment, I went to the bank and transferred the amount that the school needed urgently, but I agonized with the guilty thought like

Jonah. I was running away in disobedience to God's commands. I could not sleep.

Early the next morning, two of my friends invited me to join and pray with them at a church in the countryside. It was a spur-of-the-moment outing. The lush greens of late summer covered the mountains and fields with blinding beauty, but my heart was in a knot.

The pastor of that church welcomed us and sat in front of us with a chalkboard. I was perplexed, thinking, 'We came here to pray.' He wrote the word "calling" on the board, and slowly began to speak.

"Land needs weeds. When you weed rice paddies, you realize that weeds are beneficial. No matter how dense the weeds may be, you cannot use herbicides to get rid of them. The weeds seem rampant at first, but come autumn, the weeds rot into fertilizer, and the land becomes rich. Trees planted in fertile lands with dense weeds grow to become giant trees. And in the areas surrounding the giant trees, weeds do not grow. It is because of the shadows from giant trees' shadows."

His inadvertent words contained a profound meaning. Those who opposed us were in fact serving as fertilizer so that giant trees could grow in the fertile land of Handong! *"Be still before the Lord and wait patiently for him; do not fret when men succeed in their ways, when they carry out their wicked schemes.... For evil men will be cut off, but those who hope in the Lord will inherit the land. A little while, and the wicked will be no more; though you look for them, they will not be found" (Psalm 37:7-10).*

He opened his Bible to Genesis Chapter 22, where Abraham was told to sacrifice his son Isaac, whom he received at the age of 100.

"Everyone who has accepted Jesus Christ and has been saved has a calling. Just as God asked Abraham for Isaac, He wants to see faith from those whom He called. We too have an Isaac. What does Isaac signify? My Isaac is my treasure, that which I cannot give up with ease. What is your Isaac?"

I shrank from his eyes, that seemed fixed on me.

"Mrs. Kim, when God asked Abraham to sacrifice his only son Isaac, do you think it was easy or difficult to do?"

I lowered my head. Thinking of KAIST and our retirement fund, I barely answered, "Difficult."

My friends also answered, "Difficult."

"But, there is a way to sacrifice with ease."

I lifted my head and looked at him.

"If you don't think of it as yours, then it's easy!"

At that instant, tears filled my eyes.

"Yes! Our health, our degrees, our jobs. God has given all these things to us."

He continued to speak.

"Telling Abraham to sacrifice Isaac – which he could not possibly do on his own – was a test from God. The moment Abraham lifted his hand with a knife pointing at Isaac, the test ended. And when the test ended, God gave Isaac back to Abraham. 'Abraham, I now know that you fear Me!'"

Tears streamed down my face. Was today's outing for my sake? After he finished speaking, he gave each of us a passage from the Bible to read. Mine was from John 21:6-18.

Jesus appeared to Peter, who had not caught any fish, and said, "Throw the net to the right side of the boat. There you will find fish."

When they did, they caught so many fish that they could not lift the net. Peter had cast his net all night but had not been able to catch even one fish! Just like Peter holding onto an empty net, we had worked night and day to find money for the school without success.

I continued to read the Word with tears in my eyes. *Again Jesus said, "Simon son of Jonah, do you truly love me?" He answered, "Yes, Lord, you know that I love you." Jesus said, "Take care of my sheep." (John 21:16).*

As I read these words, God's voice filled my heart.

"My beloved daughter, do you love Me? Do you truly love the students of Handong?"

I answered just as Peter did.

"Lord, You know that I love You, and You know how much I love the students of Handong."

"Then, offer Me your retirement fund. Let Me use it for them!"

God wanted to correct my selfish heart. I began to cry. My friends had not realized how the Holy Spirit had moved my heart. When I came outside, I called Young-Gil.

"Today, I understood God's will. Do as you please."

"Hallelujah! You are a woman of prayer. Thank you."

Young-Gil immediately called a friend at KAIST and said, "Please process my resignation today and transfer my severance pay to Handong's account."

That evening, I confessed, "Young-Gil, I had been anxious at times with the fear that God would no longer take responsibility for our future. Ridicules, insults, persecutions, indictments, lawsuits, and endless worries about finances – whenever things got rough, KAIST had always been my secret refuge. When that door was shut forever today, I could finally see the true refuge."

I realized that I had proudly and secretly depended on Young-Gil's successful research career more than I had on God. I had not understood that God had given him such a successful career for a greater purpose. I prayed with Young-Gil, "Lord, forgive me for trusting only in what I could see with my own eyes. Thank You that You have brought my secret refuge out in the open. I now want to enter the true refuge that You have prepared for me. It is an unseen path, but I want to follow trusting only You."

When I walked along the visible and safe path, I was bold. But when I walked on the path that I could not see, I was filled with doubts and fears. It was because I did not know God's purpose. God always trains those whom he called for His purpose to be separated from the things of the world.

I slowly began to develop immunity to God's training. In truth, I felt freedom for the first time in a long while, and I was finally happy. From that moment on, I started to regain the weight I had lost. *"As for me, it is good to be near God. I have made the Sovereign Lord my refuge; I will tell of all your deeds"* *(Psalm 73:28).*

Honesty is the Best Policy

When we had given up securing a bank loan, a manager from a bank came to the school. Young-Gil explained the school's difficult financial situation in detail. After he left, Vice President Oh said, "President Kim! If you want to secure a loan, you have to leave out some of the disadvantageous facts. I now wonder if the bank will agree to give us the loan. If they do, then it is by God's grace."

160

A few days later, the bank called. "Our bank has decided to approve the loan."

"God, thank you!"

The school now had some breathing room. *"No temptation has seized you except what is common to man. And God is faithful; he will not let you be tempted beyond what you can bear. But when you are tempted, he will also provide a way out so that you can stand up under it" (I Corinthians 10:13).*

A few years later, the head of that bank, who is now an adjunct professor at Handong, told us the behind-the-scenes story at the time of the loan approval.

"Most people only talk of things that would help them in the loan approval process. President Kim, however, talked of his school's circumstances with such candor that my team reported that they had even greater trust in him despite some of the adverse conditions for the loan. I agreed with them, so we approved the loan."

Young-Gil liked to use the phrase, "Honesty is the best policy."

One day, I asked Young-Gil, "Which is more painful for you, the school not having enough money, or going to court with indictments and lawsuits?"

"The school not having enough money is definitely more difficult. The indictments affect only me, but the school's money problems afflict all Handong students!"

Young-Gil prayed the prayer of Agur: *"Two things I ask of you, O Lord; do not refuse me before I die: Keep falsehood and lies far from me; give me neither poverty nor riches, but give me only my daily bread. Otherwise, I may have too much and disown you and say, 'Who is the Lord?' Or I may become poor and steal, and so dishonor the name of my God" (Proverbs 30:7-9).*

President Kim! Your Socks are Inside Out!

In May 1999, the deadline for repaying $500,000 for the construction of the women's dormitory approached. The construction company had done its best to delay the deadline, and the school could not ask for another extension. Returning from an unsuccessful fund-raising trip to Seoul, Young-Gil walked back and forth in his office all day in urgent prayer. When evening came, he was in despair.

The next day, Pastor T. Bahn, who was on campus as a guest speaker for the chapel, visited Young-Gil's office. Young-Gil exchanged hellos with Pastor Bahn, but his mind was elsewhere. Pastor Bahn, then, said, "President Kim, one of your socks is inside out. You must have another emergency on your mind."

Young-Gil looked down at his socks. One was black, and the other was in the reverse side, with loose, white stitches sticking out. Young-Gil had not planned on explaining the school's urgent situation to Pastor Bahn, but at that moment, he asked the pastor to pray for the school.

"Pastor Bahn, if we do not find $500,000 by tomorrow, then the school will be in default. We have overcome many obstacles until now by God's grace, but we don't have any recourse right now. My heart is so heavy. Please pray for us."

After thinking for a while, Pastor Bahn said, "I know a businessman in Incheon. Would you like me to ask him for help?"

"Yes, please try," Young-Gil asked.

It was already near the close of business hours, and the businessman was out of the office. They waited anxiously for a return call, which finally came. Pastor Bahn explained the school's financial difficulties to him. He replied that he would do his best but said that securing $500,000 by tomorrow would not be easy given his relatively poor cash flow at that moment. However, Young-Gil thanked God for being able to spend the night with a hope. Praying all night and unable to sleep, Young-Gil called Vice President Oh in the morning.

"Please go to Seoul tomorrow and wait there."

This request was made to process the paperwork as soon as the money came through. After telling Jesus that the feast had run out of wine, Mary waited in silence for Jesus to act. Just like Mary, we too waited in silence, holding our breath. Thinking that the school might in fact be forced to go under that day, I said to Young-Gil as he left the house in the morning, "Young-Gil, people say 'man proposes, God disposes.' You'll lose your health if you are always under stress like this. Handong is God's university, so God will be even more troubled than us if it goes into bankruptcy. It's not your fault."

When Jesus was about to return to Judea in order to raise Lazarus from the dead, the disciples tried to stop Him, saying, *"Rabbi," they said, "a short while ago the Jews tried to stone you, and yet you are going back there?"*

"Lazarus is dead, and for your sake I am glad I was not there, so that you may believe. But let us go to him.

Then Thomas said to the rest of the disciples, "Let us also go, that we may die with him" (John 11:8-16).

"We'll just return to Judea with Jesus and be stoned to death." Thomas's resigned and his unbelieving attitude reflected his inability to overcome the fear of death. He had not realized that Jesus is the resurrection and the life.

I was like Thomas. I had resigned myself to bankruptcy, telling myself that there was nothing to be done. How could we borrow $500,000 from a man that we had never met and was having poor cash flow? The road ahead was not only unseen, but covered with heavy fog that made it impossible to see to the left or right. That evening, when Young-Gil came home, I asked, "What happened today?" Young-Gil's eyes quickly filled with tears as he looked at me. He ran to the bathroom to wash his face. He then told me the whole story. He had waited all morning for a phone call, and the call finally came from the businessman.

"At 2 pm, I will wire transfer $500,000 to the school."

My heart swelled as I listened to Young-Gil.

"My goodness! God even knows that you had one sock on inside out!"

Our God even knows all the hairs on our heads! This is not an exaggeration. The omniscient God who knows the clothes we are wearing today, down to our socks, is my protector! For the first time in a long while, I was finally able to lay down all my sorrows and anxieties and take comfort in God. *"Indeed, the very hairs of your head are all numbered. Don't be afraid; you are worth more than many sparrows" (Luke 12:7).*

I no longer needed to ask, "Lord, where are You?" Even if I was standing at the edge of a cliff, He would be right behind me, holding me with His strong arms. Pastor Bahn, who had briefly visited Handong, and the businessman were like Mary, a guest at

Can's wedding feast that ran out of wine. God works through our co-workers who care about others' concerns as their own. But I still said to God in sad protest, "God, couldn't You have given it to us in advance if You were going to give it anyway? Why do You give it to us after we've gone through such a wait that is so draining for us?"

"If I had given it to you in advance, would you have prayed?"

"You're right, God. We've lost too much credibility with You."

"Remember how the Lord your God led you all the way in the desert these 40 years, to humble you and to test you in order to know what was in your heart, whether or not you would keep his commands. He humbled you, causing you to hunger and then feeding you with manna, which neither you nor your fathers had known, to teach you that man does not live on bread alone but on every word that comes from the mouth of the Lord"
(Deuteronomy 8:2-3).

Tomorrow will Worry about Itself

As I headed towards a Methodist church to give a testimony, I worried about whether the congregation had seen the previous night's news. The night before, on October 25, 2000, all the evening news programs broadcasted without restraint the prosecution's indictment. The prosecutor sought four years in prison for Young-Gil and two and a half years for Vice President Oh for the alleged embezzlement of school funds. My heart was heavy as I wondered if people could be moved by a testimony of the wife of such a President. While driving on the freeway to the church, my phone rang. Young-Gil's voice was grave.

"Young-Ae, something terrible has happened. We need $1 million by tomorrow and $400,000 by Monday – a total of $1.4 million. Otherwise, the school will go under. Our creditors saw the news last night, and they want payment on their notes immediately even though we still have three months until the due dates. They are saying that they don't want notes outstanding on a school where the President has been indicted. I can't get in touch with Mr. H. Kang of our board member, so check on his phone numbers for me."

We had to find $1 million in one day. Young-Gil's indictment was no longer the main problem. How could I proclaim that God is alive in a situation like this? The two Handong parents accompanying me also fell silent. Finally, I was able to get in touch with Mrs. Kang, who said, "Mrs. Kim, what can we do? He is traveling in Japan on business and won't return until tomorrow. President Kim is going through too much!"

Her voice was full of tears. Arriving at the church, I asked the pastor before he could speak, "Pastor, did you see the news last night? Do you think it's okay for me to go ahead with a testimony?"

"Mrs. Kim, we run into all kinds of difficulties when we do God's work. Don't be discouraged in any way – proclaim the Gospel with courage!"

Encouraged by his words, I stepped onto the stage and forgot all about the prosecution's seeking for a four-year prison sentence or the loans and the possibility of bankruptcy. I witnessed the God of "**But even if He does not,**" as Daniel's three friends had professed (Daniel 3:18). Such strength did not come from me. When the service ended, about 20 Handong parents from the area were waiting for me. They were all worried about the news of the night before. The pastor said, "Handong parents are worse than kindergarten parents. Since you're all gathered here, you can hold a revival meeting here."

He opened the pastor's office for us, and served us hot tea. It was late at night, but we cried out to God for the $1 million that we needed the next day and prayed for the trial.

When I got home past midnight, the whole family was waiting for me, but they did not seem worried. I wondered, "Has there been some good news?" Although nothing had happened, my family had been comforted by the Holy Spirit of peace. *"Do not be anxious about anything, but in everything, by prayer and petition, with thanksgiving, present your requests to God. And the peace of God, which transcends all understanding, will guard your hearts and your minds in Christ Jesus" (Philippians 4:6-7).*

Young-Gil suggested that we call Mr. Kim in Los Angeles, who had helped the school during the days of Korea's economic crisis with a $1 million donation. Mr. and Mrs. Kim had been a source of encouragement and strength whenever the school was in a difficult situation.

"It's the middle of the night there! What has happened?" They were surprised by the phone call. Without reservations, I explained the desperate situation to Mrs. Kim. As always, she comforted me.

"Mrs. Kim, Handong is God's university, and He won't let it go under. I can't do anything now since it's 1 o'clock in the morning in Korea, but I'll do whatever I can from here when the day breaks there. Don't worry too much, and go to sleep."

The next day was Saturday. There was no way that we could get $1 million on our own before the bank closed at 1 pm. Because of the $1 million, Young-Gil's indictment did not even enter my thoughts. We entrusted tomorrow's worries to God and went to bed. *"Therefore do not worry about tomorrow, for tomorrow will worry about itself. Each day has enough trouble of its own" (Matthew 6:34).*

At 9 am the next day, there was a phone call from the United States.

"Mrs. Kim, we were only able to secure $300,000 because of the limited time. I think we'll have to borrow a little from here and there within Korea."

Mrs. Kim from Los Angeles had been busy working to find a way. While Young-Gil was on the phone trying to borrow money, 11 o'clock passed. I became nervous. Then, the phone rang.

"Mrs. Kim, we just wired $1 million to the school's account."

It was Mrs. Kim from Los Angeles. Hallelujah! Our prayers had been answered. Young-Gil and I were once again touched by the hand of God. *"But who am I, and who are my people, that we should be able to give as generously as this? Everything comes from you, and we have given you only what comes from your hand" (I Chronicles 29:14).*

Later that day, Mr. Kang called upon his return from his trip to Japan.

"Mrs. Kim, what happened to the loan situation?"

I met them and told them of the wonderful works of God. After hearing the details, Mr. Kang's eyes were filled with tears. He said:

"But Mrs. Kim, I have a question that I ask myself. I thought carefully about whether my heart for Handong would remain the same even after President Kim's retirement. Honestly speaking, I can't help but think that my heart comes from my personal relation-ship with you and President Kim."

I lifted up a quick prayer for wisdom. The following verse came to mind: *"Each one should use whatever gift he has received to serve others, faithfully administering God's grace in its various forms" (I Peter 4:10).*

"Mr. Kang, of course God uses our personal relationships, but we are God's administrators. For whom does the administrator exist? He exists for God, who is his Lord. I believe that God's attention is on our students. We are merely tools that are being used for Handong students. Our task is to be the students' coaches and supporters. John the Baptist was also satisfied with the joy of being the messenger who introduced the bridegroom Jesus. You can support Handong students with your possessions, and we can train them as President and professor. It is our privilege and honor to look to the roles that our Handong students will play in the days ahead! My heart jumps at such a thought."

Handong's Mirages

A danger of the desert is mirages. Walking through the desert under the burning sun without a drop of water, the traveler cannot see even a few feet ahead because of the sandstorms. He is about to collapse as his strength gives out. At that moment when the dust storm calms down, he sees something in the distance – an oasis! A vast lake with calm water reflecting the sky as far away as the eyes can see! New strength rises from within, and he thinks that thirst, hunger, heat, and fear will all disappear in that place. But it is only a mirage.

In our path through the desert, several mirages appeared.

The First Mirage: $100 Million

In the spring of 1999, a visitor came to the school.

"A man who owns about $100 million worth of real estate in Seoul wants to donate his entire fortune to education rather than leaving it as inheritance to his children. When I told him about Handong, he seemed very interested and wanted to visit the school in person."

Our hearts began to pound. But the man with $100 million delayed his visit for over six months. Summer passed and autumn arrived. Around the fall harvest festival, on the day when the elderly gentleman was scheduled to visit the school, we were busy with preparations to welcome him. Even the Chairman of board and his wife cancelled their plans to be present. When the guest arrived, Young-Gil briefed him on the school's financial situation and its development strategy and plans. The gentleman, who was 72 years old, listened without any response.

"He must be very careful with words," I thought.

After the meeting, Vice President Oh went to Seoul several times with the necessary paperwork to complete the donation process. Vice President Oh spent many days requiring incredible patience. Some days, he would sit in a café with the silent donor before returning empty-handed. Then, one day, when the elderly gentleman requested payment for fees related to the transaction, we began to have doubts. Did he really have all the money? No one wanted to say it out loud, but we were all uncomfortable.

One day in October, Vice President Oh and Handong's finance officer went to the district office to look into zoning issues for the land that the donor had listed. When they came back, they looked at us and shook their heads. What we had feared was true. All the pieces of land on the donor's list belonged to other people. After hearing the story, Pastor Ha smiled and said, "Imposters aren't just attracted to rich people; they're even more attracted to desperate people who will hold onto straws."

The Second Mirage: Germanium

In the winter of 2000, Pastor S. Kim, one of the members of Board of Trustee, who had been hospitalized after a heart surgery, wanted to see us right away. When we arrived at the hospital, Pastor Kim introduced us to the patient in the bed next to his. His excited voice was unbefitting a man who had just gone through a heart surgery.

"This man owns mountainous land in the central region of Korea, and he says that it's not just an ordinary mountain. Please listen to his story."

The man said, "My mountain is covered with germanium rocks. On a rainy day, the water from the mountains almost purifies the sewage in the stalls of the village at the base of the mountain. The village folks who drink the water from my mountain are younger and healthier than others, and their gray hair even turns back to black. We have solicited several Research Labs, but I'd like Handong to look into the germanium in our mountain, so we can develop this together."

Pastor Kim, lying in a hospital bed with bandages around his chest, thought only about Handong's financial troubles. That evening, Young-Gil researched information on germanium on the Internet. If only it was a germanium-covered mountain! A few days later, he visited the mountain with a Handong professor. Full of expectation, they carefully climbed the mountain, which was still covered with ice. They collected rock samples and sent them to KAIST and several other research labs for analysis.

While waiting for the lab results, we imagined "what-if" scenarios. What if it truly were germanium? The school would no longer have to worry about money! I laughed out loud just thinking about it. I looked at a rock sample, which resembled a plain piece of granite. Would this piece of rock yield magic that would guarantee health? Young-Gil placed the rock in a glass jar of water and drank from it every morning.

"The water tastes good," he said.

Perhaps, Young-Gil wanted to believe it was true. Then came the lab results.

"No trace of germanium found on the rock samples."

We learned to be thankful even for our mirages. They had strengthened us to travel this far without giving up. After several mirages, God directed us to a real oasis. The Bible compares Christian living with a battle and calls us to fight a good fight of faith. Rather than guaranteeing lives of comfort, Jesus promised His disciples the cross and said that victory would surely follow after the good fight. *"Weeping may remain for a night, but rejoicing comes in the morning" (Psalm 30:5).*

God allowed trials and tribulations in our lives. Amidst inconceivable financial pressure, persecution, and hardship, we learned to trust God and no one else – not ourselves, not other people. When we stood in despair, God did not change the painful circumstances but instead showed us His faithfulness, so that we could overcome what lay before us. Through many incidences, God proved clearly that He would never disappoint us and would always keep His promise. *"I ask you, therefore, not to be discouraged because of my sufferings for you, which are your glory" (Ephesians 3:13).*

CHAPTER 10:

Even If Surrounded By Enemies

The Gates of Hell Cannot Overcome Hyoam Chapel

On February 23, 1999, we celebrated the completion of Hyoam Chapel.

**University Chapel "Hyoam" dedicated on Feb. 23, 1999,
for worship service and spiritual education center.**

Even in the chilly air of early spring, the Handong family was full of joy. The chapel had been built with white granite that looked as if it had descended from heaven. We were thankful to see its wide, long staircase, the beautiful glass café facing the chapel, and the cross that stood tall in the middle. We had endured many obstacles after spending the $2 million donation as collateral for a loan, but it was finally completed after three years of heartaches.

When the school first opened, we had made a temporary sanctuary by tearing down the wall between two lecture halls. We purchased a grand piano with the donations of a few professors, and our students excitedly carried it up the stairs to the fourth floor chapel. We were as excited as newlyweds preparing a home.

The temporary chapel had been our place of worship for four years. During the second year, as the number of students increased, we had chapel service twice on Wednesday due to our limited space. Our chapel was always filled with the passionate excitement of our students. On the front wall between two large windows, hung a thin, wooden cross from Jesus Abbey, the only physical indication that this room was a chapel.

Below the fragile, wooden cross was a low platform stage of lively worship led by teams of professors and students. The crooked cross made of acacia wood seemed to foreshadow the narrow, winding path of affliction that lay ahead. But its power did not lie in its appearance. *"For the message of the cross is foolishness to those who are perishing, but to us who are being saved it is the power of God. For it is written: "I will destroy the wisdom of the wise; the intelligence of the intelligent I will frustrate"* (I Corinthians 1:18-19).

The cross of Hyoam Chapel could be seen from the school's entrance gates. It was a symbol that announced Handong as God's university. A university chapel that the gates of Hell could not overcome had been finally completed (Matthew 16:18). During the chapel dedication service, the guest speaker who was also the parent of a Handong student, said,

"Just like a painting is complete only when the artist throws the last stroke, today's chapel dedication announces to the world that the painting of Handong is now completed. It also signifies that Handong's struggles are nearing to an end. When we watch a sporting event that we have already won being replayed on TV, we do not need to be nervous or anxious because we know that we have won. Likewise, today's service is a flare that signals the end of Handong's long struggle. I am assured that God will bring Handong to victory.

We have completed the hardware by building the chapel, and now we must complete the invisible software and recover true worship. I pray that this church will become one of unceasing prayers, a church of the highest praise, a church of living words.

Handong Global University must witness to the world that God is alive, and how He has worked through it. Our God who blessed those who loved Jerusalem will also bless Handong Global University."

Leaders are not born, but Made

The historical first commencement, producing "History Makers", was held in Feb. 24 1999 as a worship service full of thanks and tears. World-class multinational companies employed these HGU graduates, and they received favorable evaluations from their superiors for their technical competence, cooperative spirit, and honest moral character.

On the eve of the school's first commencement, students gathered to celebrate. The first graduating class of 1999 did not want to end their four years at Handong with the graduation ceremony alone. The students spent the whole night with professors and younger classmates sharing their Handong memories and their dreams. The students wholeheartedly praised the living and faithful God, whom they had thoroughly experienced at Handong.

The long-awaited shower poured on the land that had barely endured the long, dry winter. Only those who witnessed the tear-filled history of Handong and its struggle for survival can understand the true meaning of this refreshing rain.

The struggle was ignited by Handong's declaration to be a genuine God's university. It was a path full of irrepressible attacks and desperate prayers in response. And on the first graduation ceremony, there were showers of blessing.

When Young-Gil stood before the graduating class, he could not start his speech as his eyes were filled with tears. I could only imagine that he was overcome by deep emotions accumulated over the past four years that he toiled with the students. Finally, he cleared his throat.

**The first historical commencement of Handong
on Feb.24, 1999 as a worship service full of thanks and tears.**

"As the first class, you have sacrificed and borne so much hardship and suffering at this new university. However, those sacrifices can be considered a privilege for you to have taken part in God's special plan to make you global Christian leaders that this era needs.

I want to ask of you three things: First, welcome new challenges. An easy, comfortable environment does not produce strong and able soldiers. Leaders are not born, but made. I pray that you will be victorious when you face hardships and challenges, with the skills that you have polished and faith in our Lord God Creator.

Second, live out a clear purpose-driven life. Allocate time for self-reflection in this world, which pushes you to run forward aimlessly. I hope you will steadfastly review and hold onto your first vision and goal in life.

Third, invest in things that are eternal, in Jesus Christ and His Kingdom. God is still searching for Christian leaders who revere the Lord and are merciful to their neighbors. Handong will continue to produce such people. I pray that you leave Handong with God, who walks with you until the ends of the earth."

All who were present in the ceremony extended their arms toward the graduating class and blessed them with songs. Eyes were moist and we could taste heaven as we gave glory to God. Since then, Young-Gil has given similar advice to each graduating class. On that day, sitting in my seat among parents, graduates, and the students, I reflected upon the opening ceremony of the school that I attended four years earlier when these graduating students had entered the school. Those graduates were the first batch of the precious refined metal from the blast furnace of Handong. They all have gone through the intense fire and heat that they endured and were broken. They were the God's people ready to be used by Him to change the world. How many sleepless nights we had spent for the reward? I prayed myself in tears, "Thank you Jesus."

The Croaking Sounds of a Bull Frog

April 16, 1999 was the day for the trial of the civil lawsuit that had begun three years before. The fate of the school depended on the results of the trial. If we lose, Handong would become a mere community university. The professors fasted and prayed, and students and parents all over the country as well as Handong supporters at home and abroad, lifted up desperate prayers. That afternoon, Young-Gil's voice over the telephone sounded somewhat down.

"Young-Ae! We need to pray a lot. There are rumors everywhere that the school is in a disadvantageous position."

The night before, I read a chapter titled 'In the Valley of Loss' in "Hinds' Feet on High Places" by Hannah Hurnard. (Barbour 2000). It was about the moment when the protagonist, a cowardly deer, was shaking in devastating fear after losing all that he had. I had a presentiment that such a crisis would come upon us as well. What if God asks, "Will you be able to accept the pain that I have chosen for you? Will you still trust and love Me?"

When Young-Gil came home after work, his face was grim.

"Attorney Lee said that we may have to postpone tomorrow's trial, so we filed for a continuance, but it was rejected. To prepare for the worst, I had a professor in the Law Department explain everything to the professors so that they won't be disappointed. I imagine that some people already have a hunch."

I calmed my heart and said to Young-Gil, "When a potter throws his pot on the ground and breaks it into pieces, he can still remake his pot. No matter what happens, let's not doubt that the providence of God, the potter, is present here. We have seen God's presence first-hand until now! The rest of our lives will be too short to tell about all that we have experienced!"

It seemed like we would lose the trial, but I encouraged my husband with the energy that I did not know I could muster. When he went into his study without supper, I cried out to God.

"Lord! I know that You always have ways of revealing Your glory no matter what the circumstance may be, but how can we watch our students, parents, and professors shaken in fear, even if it's for a short while? How can we shut our ears to those who mock us and say, 'Where is your God now?' God! Do You really have to make us go through this?"

Tears poured out of my eyes. *"So give your servant a discerning heart to govern your people and to distinguish between right and wrong. For who is able to govern this great people of yours?" (I Kings 3:9).*

At that moment, the phone rang. It was the energetic voice of an alumnus.

"Mrs. Kim! The alumni in Seoul have gathered together to pray for tomorrow's trial. God will surely be on our side. Victory is ours."

A little while later, there was another phone call. It was from a senior student at Handong.

"Mrs. Kim, you must be praying a lot. All of us in our dormitory are praying together. God will give us victory."

I thought about the shock that the students would receive, and I felt that I needed to say something.

"Absolutely! Even if there are difficulties along the way, the final result will surely be a blessing. We'll know everything tomorrow, but just in case... Even if we do not get the result that we expect tomorrow, you will still believe that God works everything out for the best, right? We should never resent God in any way!"

"Mrs. Kim, why do you say such words of unbelief?"

"Didn't I say just in case?"

After a moment, he must have realized what was going on. He said with maturity, "If President Kim can withstand everything as our leader, then we can surely endure anything." I swallowed my tears. If we lost the trial the next day, there was going to be a lot of confusion at the school. I shook with fear as I wondered whether we could handle the chaos. Ominous rumors abounded – that the preparation to take over the school was complete, that government-appointed directors were about to be sent. Yet, we were only pots that the potter had made. *"But the pot he was shaping from the clay was marred in his hands; so the potter formed it into another pot, shaping it as seemed best to him" (Jeremiah 18:4).*

Sometime later, Young-Gil came out of his study and said, "Young-Ae, I think the school is going to win. After praying, I have unfathomable peace in my heart. As I looked back, I remembered hearing that the court usually accepts a request for continuance from the side who is at a disadvantage. Since they didn't accept our request today, I think we're going to win. I'm sure I'm right."

His words befitted the eternally optimistic man he is, and I felt pity and compassion. Young-Gil recovered his energy.

At 10:15 am the next morning, the phone began to ring.

"Mrs. Kim, we won! Hallelujah!"

"We won!"

"Mrs. Kim, you heard, right? We won, we won!"

"We won!" The students shouted out victory throughout the campus. Some students rushed into Young-Gil's office in excitement.

"President Kim! We heard the news!"

We all cried out in pure joy and we thanked God. *"If the Lord had not been on our side when men attacked us, when their anger flared against us, they would have swallowed us alive; the flood would have engulfed us, the torrent would have swept over us, the raging waters would have swept us away. Praise be to the Lord, who has not let us be torn by their teeth. We have escaped like a bird out of the fowler's snare; the snare has been broken, and we have escaped. Our help is in the name of the Lord, the Maker of heaven and earth" (Psalm 124:2-8).*

They said that this civil lawsuit trial was the biggest ever conducted in local courts of this region. They said that previous judges who had been a part of the court system did not want to preside over this case. God had prepared righteous judges and had led Handong to safety. *"Do not show partiality in judging; hear both small and great alike. Do not be afraid of any man, for judgment belongs to God. Bring me any case too hard for you, and I will heart it" (Deuteronomy 1:17).*

One of the professors told us a story that day.

"Late last night as I was leaving my office, I heard sounds that resembled the croaking of bullfrogs. I walked over to where the sound was coming from, and I stopped dead in my tracks. The sounds were prayers of students spread throughout the lecture hall. They were on their knees on the cold hallway floors in front of the President's Office. At that moment, I was so ashamed of myself. I thought about how little I had prayed for the school as a professor compared to our students."

Handong is founded on the name of our God and countless prayers, and it will not fall even when the rain pours and the floods come and the winds blow against it - just like the house built on a rock!

The long, bitter winter of Handong was finally passing.

Internal Division to Mold 'Broken Hearts'

Thirty-two thousand men followed Gideon to fight against the Midianites, but the number was too big in God's eyes. God ordered Gideon to reduce the number to 300. The men of Ephraim who could not participate in the battle bitterly complained to Gideon. The Israelites won the war, but dissension began among the Israelites. *"Now the Ephraimites asked Gideon, 'Why have you treated us like this? Why didn't you call us when you went to fight Midian?' And they criticized him sharply" (Judges 8:1).*

When the school finally won the long legal battle and opposition outside the school began to subside, problems began to arise from within the school. A few students began to criticize the school, and some professors voiced opinions that sounded good on the surface, but ended up causing discord. Soon people were getting hurt. Such negative displays were reflections of our unbroken hearts. This was why God called us – such feeble but arrogant beings – to the desert school of Handong: He wanted us, with our sinful natures, to collide with each other and become broken! Our pains and hardship came about because our focus was not on God where it should be, but on ourselves instead.

One Sunday, I reflected on these things while listening to a pastor's sermon, "The Scene Inside Noah's Ark."

"During the time of Noah, God was in despair over men's evil, but Noah stood out in God's eyes because he was different from the rest. Human beings all have a desire to be recognized, and Noah was no different. If Noah had not obeyed God and built the ark, he would not have been mocked by those around him. So, where did he get the courage to obey? Noah was able to do so because of the glorious light of God that came into Noah's spirit. He was connected to God at all times, 24 hours a day. That is why he was called righteous by God.

"By obeying God, Noah must have experienced bitter spiritual struggles and loneliness. Those who want to obey God will be ridiculed and persecuted by the world. But amidst all the mockery, he quietly built the ark under the dry sky that had no sign of rain. Noah endured the world's persecution by honoring God with his whole heart.

Think about the scene inside, when the door closed on the ark that had been being built for over 120 years. The hedgehog, who pierces all those around him whenever he moves with sharp needles that stick out from his body; the woodpecker, who talks incessantly; the skunk, who needs to be isolated because of his foul smell; the giant elephant, who inconveniences all those around him with his massive size; and the peacock, who thinks he is a prince above everyone else. All these different animals with their unique personalities had to share their lives in a common space, but they could not just tell someone to go outside the ark because they did not like him. Just as on an airplane where we cannot tell an annoying child to go play outside, we must learn to live together and love each other inside the ark. We sing the song that says 'How beautiful the image of God that we see in our brothers,' but often we are like the skunk who criticizes the hedgehog. We must learn to adjust our characters by learning to live with each other within our communities."

In order to develop our students' characters, we implemented a system of teams in the early days of Handong. Students and professors maintain close relationships within a team, and they become one as the professors become the students' advisors and mentors. The team system is a source of pride for Handong, but because of the close relationship between the students and the professors, sometimes students – either accidentally or intentionally - ended up learning facts about the school administration that only professors should know. Both good and bad, rumors spread among the students, which were then used by some outsiders for malicious purposes. Some students raised objections to the school's identity and leadership, sometimes based on misinformation and other times as constructive criticism.

PART III: SACRIFICE

CHAPTER 11:

The God of Comfort
Who Opens Prison Doors

IMPRISONMENT

Due to the university's financial hardship, and because of the IMF(International Monetary Fund) turmoil in Korea in 1997, there was no money for the school to pay professors' salaries. At that time, the Ministry of Education of the Korean Government recognized Handong's achievement of academic reform for the 21st century, and the school received US $3.4 million in three years. Due to its financial deficiency, the university used the money to pay the professors' back salaries in December 1997, and reimbursed the funds according to their original designation the following month. This gave our local opponents a good excuse in the attempt to topple young-Gil from the position of Handong Global University's president. In May 2000, they accused him of misusing the government funds. The local court's verdict was guilty, and he was arrested at the courthouse and put into prison on May 11, 2001. The arrest of an active university president at a court was a historically unprecedented event.

When the judge in the local court had finished reciting the verdict on May 11, 2001 and asked if Young-Gil had anything to say, he could not think of anything for a while. He just stared blankly at the judge. His mind was stupefied, and he could not comprehend what the verdict meant: 'Embezzlement,' 'Risk of tampering with the evidence,' 'Intentional avoidance of court appearance without just cause,' Before he could think, the correctional officers came in and took him through the court's back doors. Once he stepped out through the doors, they put handcuffs on him. When he felt the cold handcuffs on his wrists, reality finally hit him.

While he was led to the prison, he closed his eyes and thought about what God's will might be through this unbelievable, helpless situation. The only thing that came into his mind was how shocked all his beloved family, students, professors, and student's parents would be. All of a sudden, he was at a complete loss. He did not even know what he was supposed to ask of God.

After being signed into the prison office, he was led to the newcomers' admissions room. He took off all his clothes and put them in a sack, and he picked up a brown prison uniform from a pile in a corner under their order. Because the pants that he had picked up were so big, he bent over to look for a smaller one, but the guard said, "Just wear anything! They're all the same, so there's no point in choosing." He also put on the white rubber shoes placed in front of his feet.

"Take off your glasses! Prison rules do not allow metal-framed glasses. Tell your family to bring you plastic-rimmed glasses when they visit you."

He held up a board that said "Number 433" and was photographed standing in front of a wall, facing forward and sideways. It was the so-called mug shot for the criminal records. Wearing clothes that had belonged to a stranger, he didn't have any thoughts or feelings. After getting his glasses confiscated, everything looked hazy. Holding a plastic spoon and two bowls that the guard had issued to him, he followed the guard to the cell to which he was assigned.

When he entered the cell, he saw several faces of those sitting inside, as if behind a thick fog. All their eyes were upon him. At that moment, someone said in a loud, angry voice, "Turn around and sit facing the wall!"

He did not know why, but he sat facing the wall for a long time. He found out later that it was part of being initiated into a room. After a long time, he heard the same voice again.

"Now turn around, and tell us your name, address, occupation, the nature of your crime, and your prior record – in the order as it reads on this piece of paper."

So he turned around, and after saying "hello" in a loud voice to everyone in the cell, he introduced himself according to the list, including the nature of his crime. As they were listening to his story, they began to comment, "That doesn't sound like something you should be arrested for. Something sounds wrong. They arrested an acting university president even before the final verdict had been reached? That seems unfair!"

They had their own interpretation regarding his crime. Then, another voice said loudly, "That Handong Global University is a problematic school!"

They all seemed as knowledgeable about the law as any attorney did. Then, a man who appeared to be the leader in the cell asked, "President, have you had lunch?"

He had skipped lunch. It was already past 4 o'clock in the afternoon.

"Hey, give him that piece of bread!"

I asked him later, "Did you eat that bread? You could eat in that situation?"

"Of course, it was very good. I was hungry." he smiled. I did not know whether to smile or to cry, thinking of how he could have had the peace of mind to eat in such a situation.

The fellow cellmates were very considerate of him. There were two small tables in that room, and the cell leader allowed him to put his bowls on one of the tables. They also exempted him from clean-up duties. At 9 pm, it was time to sleep. He wondered how all these men could sleep in such a small room. Each person rolled his blanket into a pillow, and 35 men were arranged in order. Every other man laid down with his head facing the other way, and they were all lying on their sides so that all of their noses almost touched the feet of the men lying next to them literally like sardines in a can.

"You may be No. 8! If you were to be placed according to when you were admitted here, you'd be last and sleeping next to the bucket (toilet bowl), so be grateful for your promotion."

Prison rules dictated that they sleep with the lights on. With such bright lights above them, they seemed to have a difficult time falling asleep. Perhaps out of boredom, since everyone was lying down yet awake, the room leader said, "Let's each talk about what we've been through in the outside world."

Everyone talked about how they had regretted their lives – how they shouldn't have done this or that. Finally, it came to his turn.

"I don't have much to say, but could I sing instead? My hometown is in an isolated region, now submerged by the construction of a dam. So I'm a wanderer without a hometown, and I like this song called 'The Spring of My Hometown."

"You want to sing? Go ahead."

He began to sing in a low voice a song that he learned in the elementary school as for most others.

"My hometown, a mountain village, with blooming flowers: Peach, apricot and baby azaleas...."

Soon, all others started to sing along with him. When he finished singing, someone said, "Hmm, President Kim, you sing pretty well."

The atmosphere had changed. That song most everybody learned in their elementary schools became the bond of friendship with his cellmates on that first night in prison. Even they seemed to briefly forget their depression and the fact that they were in confinement. He closed my eyes and thought about the mountains of his hometown. All of a sudden, sorrow burst inside his heart and he could not hold crying. "I'm now 62 years old. How can I be in this kind of place lying like this now?" They laid next to each other, their clothes and their flesh almost touching, with their breath so close to each other's that they couldn't tell whether it was his own or someone else's. Lying down in that cell bursting with 35 men placed side by side, he stood before God, as a bare naked soul.

He didn't know what to think for a couple of days. He was in a prison that he hadn't even seen in his dreams. He realized that a prison, too, was a world of its own with real people living in, and that it was a bearable place. Each person in that place was born with a precious life, and each person's life had its own circumstances, tears, sighs and sorrows that only that individual could tell. Each man was searching for his own hope.

After a week of imprisonment, he was moved to a cell with only seven people. Everyone in that cell was a newcomer, so he didn't have to go through another initiation. Only then was he able to focus on each person in his cell. He wrote out the Lord's Prayer and the Apostle's Creed for each person, and He suggested that they give thanks to God for each meal. Strangely, no one objected.

He prayed whenever someone had to appear in court. So, he was able to calm his heart and share God's grace with cell mates each day. For seven years, he hadn't had a day of rest free from worrying about money. It was nice to be able to meditate on the Bible without worrying about money after a long time. He read all the books that he hadn't been able to read before, and he had nothing to do except to pray and sing praises while he was in prison. He began to think that perhaps God was giving him a special vacation since he had been so busy until then.

He wrote down his confession in his notebook. "My spirit stands before God, shaking. I have never stood before Him like this, with absolutely nothing such as my name, honor, position, pride, pains, and anxiety. I am living the true freedom of having shed all those things. I have been running with my focus only on what is ahead, and God has now allowed me to stop for a while, and in this strange place, through this strange method, He has freed me and is meeting with me, one on one. This is my place of prayer, my attic where I meet with the Lord."

Eighteen days into my imprisonment at Kyungju Prison, on May 28, the warden came to him and said to him in a low voice, "You'll be moved to Daegu Prison in preparation for the appellate court trials there. Don't tell anyone, but get ready by 10 o'clock tomorrow morning". When he thought about leaving the next day, his heart was in turmoil over his cellmates. He realized what it meant to live together day in and day out in the same room, breathing the same air. In the morning of his departure, he desperately prayed for each person in his room. He began to cry and prayed:

"Father God, thank you for allowing us to meet here. We are in a tough place, but even a prison becomes a place of peace and thanks because You are here with us. Have mercy on them, and bless them so they may become Your children. Let them become bearers of the evidence that You are with us on this Earth. Watch over them as the apples of your eye. Please take care of their families. No matter how long they may have to stay in here, let them learn of a new life through patience, and let their days become days of growth of their faith."

They all said good-byes in tears. When he came outside with his sack, all the prisoners who were to be transferred to the Daegu Prison were lined up and roped, like a string of dead fish. His hands were cuffed and a thick rope bound him from shoulder to waist, front and back. He could hardly move because the handcuffs were so tight on his wrists, and he couldn't even lean back on his chair because of the thick rope on his back.

Then, a warden came to him and said, "President Kim, please understand. This is a rule. After an escape incident recently, our rules require us to put two handcuffs on each person." The bus left Kyungju prison and drove toward Daegu prison on Highway1. The mountains and fields were covered with lush summer green. The outside scenery was very familiar, and yet everything seemed new. He had a million emotions within him, and He began to weep. He, too, felt scorned and wronged, but it was not because of his sorrow that he cried. After being handcuffed and roped, the weight of the pain that our Lord must have had to endure was heavy upon him. His crown of thorns, the whips, the spits, the insults! His loneliness and sorrows, the shame and betrayal – Young-Gil said that he could feel all those emotions piercing his heart. Jesus Christ, who is God the Creator, came to this world as a man, and that is the culmination of humility and lowering of oneself.

"Your attitude should be the same as that of Christ Jesus: Who, being in very nature God, did not consider equality with God something to be grasped, but made himself nothing, taking the very nature of a servant, being made in human likeness. And being found in appearance as a man, he humbled himself and became obedient to death – even death on a cross!" (Philippians 2:5-8).

When he thought about how much Jesus had to lower himself, he felt everything which he was going through was nothing. God had to take a human form in order to save us, a sinner – it was the only way for forgiveness! He could feel throughout his heart and body the love

188

of God who sent His only son to die for us because nothing could be accomplished without the price of such a sacrifice. Jesus obeyed all the way to His death, and He became the way, the truth, and the life!

"For even the Son of Man did not come to be served, but to serve, and to give his life as a ransom for many" (Mark 10:45).

When he arrived at the Daegu Prison, some of the prison guards who had been reading the newspaper looked up and recognized him. "President Young-Gil Kim of Handong Global University, you are the elder who was the chairman of the Korea Association of Creation Research, right? We were just reading about you in newspapers."

They were members of a Christian group in the prison. They commented on how strange it was that the school itself had not said anything against the President even if its faculty and staff would have been the first to know if the President had truly done anything wrong. About a month after my transfer to Daegu Prison, Christian guards came to me and said, "We think that you are going to leave this place soon, and so we prepared a special event tonight. Please join us and share your testimony with us."

And, so in the Christian gathering he preached on Philippians 2:5-11. After the ceremony, they put their hands on his shoulders and prayed for him.

"We, the Church of Smyrna in this prison, send you, Elder Young-Gil Kim, as a missionary to the outside world."

Their tears fell on his shoulders and hands.

"President Kim, when you are released into the outside world, please don't forget about us, the Church of Smyrna." I still say to myself once in a while, "I'm a missionary sent by the Church of Smyrna."

The Memorable Teachers' Day

The fourth day Young-Gil was detained was Teachers' Day. At 9 am, students with carnations in their hands gathered at the school chapel. Led by two buses wrapped in banners that read "We Love You, President Kim!" and "We Love You, Vice President Oh," a total of 29 buses filled with students headed toward the prison.

**On the teacher's day of May 15, 2001, about 1,800 students
along with their parents and professors were gathered in front
of the prison gate when the president was in imprisonment.**

It all began by a group of students who suggested through Handong intranet, "Tomorrow is Teachers' Day. Following Handong's tradition of commemorating Teachers' Day, we will go to hand deliver carnation flowers to the President and Vice President and sing the 'Song for Teachers.' We will go to visit them in the prison!"

Contrary to our expectation that only a small number of students who had no class that day would go, many more decided to join as one. Some professors intentionally posted a notice "No class today. I'm not feeling well," so that students could feel free to go. The student government had to rent buses – at first 10, then 20, and finally 29, until there was no more available bus to rent in the city. The night before, some parents even traveled from another city to join the students. Altogether, about 1,800 Handong students were mobilized, moving silently in a well-organized manner. The Handong family personified silent prayer in action.

An historical procession that exceeded our imagination formed outside the prison building. The police prepared for the worst and carefully watched the procession, fully ready to respond at the first sign of disturbance. The students lined up in an orderly fashion in front of the building. Not wanting to provoke the prison guards in any way, they began to sing the "Song for Teachers" in low voices.

"A teacher's grace as high as the sky,

becoming higher and higher as we look up...."

The song turned into tears, then into outbursts of sobs. They then hummed "Amazing Grace," the hymn that their President loved the most. The hymn spoke of how we could not begin to express the amazing grace of salvation no matter how much we cry. Our students hummed this song in tears.

**Carnations piled up before the prison
gate on Teacher's day of May 15, 2001.**

Young-Gil was inside the prison building, but I knew that the song of those students whom he loved so much should have seeped into his heart. At that moment, someone hugged me from behind.

"Mrs. Kim, Mrs. Kim! People will say that we lost everything because of Jesus. I lost my son, and now President Kim is in prison. How could this happen?"

It was the mother who had lost her son four years before, the mother of Young-Min Kwon, who was killed while he had gone to Fiji on a short-term mission trip. Her pained cries enveloped me. My heart sank again.

"I came back from a trip to Europe this morning, and I came here as fast as I could when I heard about President Kim."

We buried our faces in each other's shoulders and cried for a long time. She said, "Mrs. Kim, I think God must be looking down at President Kim now and feeling sorry for him. God must be working out His amazing will in all of this. Right now it feels like we have fallen miles deep into an abyss, but God will accomplish unimaginable things through this incident as he did countless times before."

When the student leaders went inside the building for a visit, the rest of the students began to sing the "Blessing Song" with arms opened wide.

When the student leaders came back, president of the student body spoke with a composed voice:

"Everyone, our President and Vice President are both well. President Kim asked me to tell all of you not to be disturbed, but instead focus all your energies on your studies. Do not be angry toward the court for its decision, nor toward the opposing party. He believes this incident to be an opportunity for him to reflect upon himself and repent, and he would like all of us to pray in faith, agreeing that God works for the good of those who love Him, who have been called according to His purpose (Romans 8:28)."

The police must have been quite shocked by the mature attitude of our students, since they had been nervously expecting the worst but when the students retreated after the quiet demonstration, they could not find even a speck of trash on the ground. When the day's events ended, the two former student government leaders sat in a corner of the parking lot and cried bitterly, holding each other as if all their sorrow and strain had burst open.

Prayer Meetings and Petitions

In May 2001, Handong professors and students were in shock after the arrest of Young-Gil and Vice President Oh, in the court and they spontaneously assembled in the school chapel in desperate prayers. There were four prayer meetings a day, at 7 and 11 in the morning and at 5 and 10 in the evening. Professors and parents began a prayer-fast relay throughout the country. Letters of encouragement poured into the school website and other Christian websites. Friends in the United States, with whom we had lost touch for a long time began to call one after another.

I was able to discover the God who comforts even amidst the darkness that had covered our lives and hidden the light of God. *"Praise be to the God and Father of our Lord Jesus Christ, the Father of compassion and the God of all comfort, who comforts us in all our troubles, so that we can comfort those in any trouble with the comfort we ourselves have received from God" (II Corinthians 1:3-4).*

On June 4, after 23 days into the imprisonment, Handong parents, alumni, and students gathered in front of the Pohang Civic Center at 1 pm to hold a campaign titled "Setting Handong's Records Straight." Buses after buses arrived from all over the country filled with Handong parents. About 700 parents and 1,200 students organized a procession with placards that read,

"President Kim is Not That Kind of Person!"

"Free the President, Whom all Parents Respect!"

After completing the one-mile street procession, the parents converged again at Hyoam Chapel to pray. I was led to the front. Watching eyes filled with sympathy, sorrow, and inexpressible encouragement and comfort, I slowly began to speak.

"To all the parents who are here, I am truly grateful. I respect all of you for sending your precious children to this school in faith, when the school has had endless days of persecution with even the President and the Vice President being imprisoned. God tells us that our heart is where our treasure is, and I wonder if God had your children sent here because He wanted to raise you up to be our intercessors of faith.

How can anything happen to us that God has not allowed? This incident, too, has been God's will, because nothing happens by chance with God. Handong is no ordinary school. Handong is a university led by God, and I've been in the front lines witnessing countless miracles that show that God is in absolute charge of 'God's University.' Just as His word tells us to *"Carry each other's burdens, and in this way you will fulfill the law of Christ" (Galatians 6:2),* we all have our own burdens to carry in order to accomplish the will of God: Burdens of parents, burdens of professors and administrators, burdens of students, and burdens of the President. When we joyfully carry our share of these burdens, the law of Christ will be fulfilled on this earth."

The representative of the parents association gave me a large basket.

"Mrs. Kim, these are our letters of encouragement to the President."

The setting sun was painting the campus in beautiful colors as the sounds of desperate prayers of Handong parents reverberated across the campus.

From all areas of society, petitions on behalf of Young-Gil poured into the relevant government agencies. Petitions from organizations such as the Korean Council for University Education (KCUE), the Korean Private University Association (KPUA), and the Association of University and College Presidents were delivered to the courts.

Petitions poured in also from Korean emigrants living in Los Angeles, Washington, D.C., Chicago, Bangkok and other cities, and were delivered to various government agencies. Petitions from many parents, the Association of Christian Churches, and other organizations were submitted to the courts and to the Blue House, the official residence of the President of the Republic of Korea.

The mother of our son's friend from Northwestern University called after anxiously searching for ways to help us.

"Let's hold a breakfast prayer meeting with those who love President Kim."

On June 8, at 7 am, we held a breakfast prayer meeting. Over 200 guests, including Dr. Young-Woo Kang of National Council on Disability (NCD) of the U.S. government; renowned pastors from various denominations; and senior educators, legal and business leaders joined us. Everyone gave words of comfort based on love and respect, and they all prayed for a fair trial.

Visitors lined up from Seoul and from abroad. There were many whom I had never met before. Some gave books and donations. How can I write about all the countless, blessed meetings? Because of the arrests, the legal proceedings, the defamation and secret attacks, and all the other workings against Handong were exposed in the bright light of day.

And so, Calvin College established a sister relationship with Handong while its president was in prison. *"Now I want you to know, brothers, that what has happened to me has really served to advance the gospel" (Philippians 1:12).*

That autumn, the Handong faculty couple and family, who were spending their sabbatical at Calvin College in Grand Rapids, Michigan, said to us, "President Kim, because of the trials that you have endured, we have been treated with undeserved honor. When we run into Calvin professors on campus, they ask us about you and the school, showing great interest and concern. And, I think since I work for a university which could not even pay its professors, Calvin College's hospitality toward us was even more exceptional."

The next year, when we visited Calvin College, President and Mrs. Byker organized a banquet in our honor and gave us unforgettable words of encouragement.

Praying and Praising in Prison

When I went to visit Young-Gil in prison, he said to me, "I pray the prayer of Jabez several times a day. *"I pray that You would bless [Handong] and enlarge [Handong's] territory! Let Your hand be with [Handong], and keep [Handong] from harm so that [Handong] will be free from pain" (I Chronicles 4:10).* And I often sing 'The Bells of Love' – this song seems so appropriate for Handong, and so I've revised the words to fit our school. One day when I leave this place, I'd like to sing it with my fellow Handong students."

I pray to our Lord with my two hands gathered, grant us Your
   amazing grace
Enlarge Handong's territory throughout the world
Oh Lord, wash away all our iniquities with Your blood
And make us one within Your love
With faith, with hope, with love, we move forward holding hands
I pray to our Lord with my two hands gathered, grant us Your
   amazing grace
Use Handong Global University that You have prepared
Oh Lord, let the new light shine upon the darkness inside us
Let us always obey Your word
Showing patience toward one another, encouraging one
   another, loving one another
We move forward toward You
Oh Lord, the bells of Your love, the bells of love
Let them hold all of us Handong family.

Every morning, my daily schedule involved leaving Pohang and
driving 2 hours to the prison in Daegu city to visit Young-Gil. To
me, Daegu was only inches away from Pohang. Everyone traveled a
long way for just the short, five-minute visit. Handong parents came
to the prison almost every morning to serve those who came to visit
Young-Gil.

Since Christ my soul from sin set free
This world has been a Heav'n to me
And 'mid earth's sorrows and its woe
Tis Heav'n my Jesus here to know
O hallelujah, yes, 'tis Heav'n
'Tis Heav'n to know my sins forgiv'n
On land or sea, what matters where
Where Jesus is, 'tis Heaven there
(C. F. Butler, 1898)

Young-Gil was especially sensitive to the heat, and when I
thought about him enduring the heat of summer inside the prison,
I could not sleep. I did not know when the decision regarding their

bail would be reached, but I prayed that his spirit inside the prison would not tire but overflow with prayers and praises.

Pouring Comfort upon Comfort

Countless emails with messages of love for Young-Gil kept flooding in. The messages were filled with words of faith that proclaimed victory. Phone calls continued to pour in from all over the world.

"Mrs. Kim, this is your student's father in New Zealand."

It was Ambassador B. Moon, who was at that time posted in New Zealand.

"I was so shocked when I saw the news. But Mrs. Kim, when Jesus heard that his beloved Lazarus was ill, He still delayed for two days before visiting his home. It must have been a painful period of waiting for his family, but Jesus had a different purpose. He was waiting for Lazarus to die. Mrs. Kim, you feel wronged and you're in pain, but wait a little longer. I believe that God's providence is present in allowing President Kim to go to prison. Through this incident, Handong's trials will become known all over the world, and God's glory will be revealed. From afar, I send a small donation as a token of my heart to you. Please use it to cover a part of President Kim's legal expenses."

Ambassador Moon and his wife sent $10,000, which they had saved for their daughter's wedding. A few days later, I received another phone call.

"You are the wife of President Kim, yes? My daughter works as a Cathy Pacific flight attendant in Hong Kong, and after reading about President Kim in the newspaper, she felt awful about what had happened and sent me some money to be forwarded to you to be used toward his bail."

"Thank you so much. I'd really like to meet you. When she comes back to Korea, please be sure to visit us. You can give us your donation then."

In the middle of June, the Cathy Pacific stewardess and her mother visited Handong. The stewardess introduced herself.

"Mrs. Kim, I came to visit Handong once before because one of the students I tutored when I was in college applied to Handong. Ever since, I have always prayed for Handong. The school has grown so much, and I am witnessing how God is here right now."

She gave me two envelopes and said,

"Mrs. Kim, this is some money that I've put together by saving on expenses as I traveled around the world. If Handong becomes a university that reaches the world and President Kim visits all the countries I have been to with his vision for Handong, then there is no greater honor for me than that."

At the end of June 2001, I received a phone call on my way to the prison.

"Mrs. Kim, my name is J. Kim. Everyone at my company and I are praying for President Kim and Handong Global University. We have collected some support funds. It's not much, but we'd like to send it to you as a small token of encouragement."

A few days later, I met her in Seoul. "Mrs. Kim, my hometown is actually Pohang. On behalf of those from my hometown who are attacking Handong, I apologize. Please forgive them; they are doing all this because they do not know that God is a living God."

She gave me a sizable donation and encouraged me.

"God has put the heavy burden of the school's finances on President Kim's shoulders, and his name will be on the lips of men, both good and bad. But these trials will become a platform on which Handong will stand tall, and Handong's financial troubles will soon be resolved."

"He has preserved our lives and kept our feet from slipping. For you, O God, tested us; you refined us like silver. You brought us into prison and laid burdens on our backs. You let men ride over our heads; we went through fire and water, but you brought us to a place of abundance" (Psalm 66:9-12).

Young-Gil's students from his old KAIST days collected some funds and visited the prison. I asked them, "Young-Gil has become a sensational news maker. Aren't you ashamed that you are his students?"

"Mrs. Kim, we are proud of the fact that we are his students, and that will never change."

Meanwhile, some of Young-Gil's students from KAIST posted the following messages at Handong's website.

Posted by K. Paik (Professor of Material Science at KAIST): I was President Young-Gil Kim's first student when he was a KAIST professor after he returned to Korea in 1979 from the United States. I watched him for the last 20 years. He gave me much support and love until I became a KAIST professor myself as I am now.

President Kim whom I have known is a very special person. He is a person who is pure and persistent when it comes to search for a truth. Surely, he is not a person who would compromise or negotiate unrightfully for personal gain.

There are a few incidents about him that I know. Even when he was in great difficulty leading Handong, he willingly gave up the KAIST professorship and cut off opportunities to return to KAIST. He pressed me to speed up the administrative process for his termination. That was the time when Handong was in critical situation that it could not even pay salaries for its staff. He wanted to spend his own retirement fund, the result of his 17 years of service, to pay for their salaries. His love for Handong, its staff and students was extraordinary. Even though the present situation is depressing and the road ahead may look treacherous, I have no doubt that the truth will win in the end.

Glorious Prison Uniform

On June 29, 2001, the trial was held at the appellate court while Young-Gil and Vice President were still in prison. The day before, Attorney J. Lee called.

"Since he can appear in court in a suit until the final verdict is reached, please prepare a suit for him when you go to visit him today. If President Kim appears in court in a prison uniform, how will all the students, professors, and parents feel?"

However, his supporters inside the prison cautiously advised against it. "Mrs. Kim, even if he wears a suit, his hands will still be tied in ropes. President Kim is here not because of his wrongdoing but because he has carried out his duties as the school's president.

His prison uniform is actually a robe of glory. For tomorrow's court appearance, we have prepared a set of clean uniform for him."

The mother of a Handong freshman, who saw the session in the appellate court, posted a message on the school's website describing the scenes at the court.

We stood up twice.

On June 29, 2001, a large group of students' parents assembled to attend the first session of the court. In the train heading for Daegu city, everyone sat expressionlessly without a word. The professors who were riding with us were also quiet.

"Is there a session of someone important?" asked the people at the courthouse who seemed startled at the waves of the people, numbering several hundred. They were parents, professors and students, converging from all over the country. Leaving their surprised expressions behind, we rushed to the Courtroom 41 keeping our mouths tightly sealed. We were afraid that our every gestures and behaviors might interfere the session. We squeezed ourselves into the small courtroom in order to allow as many people as possible to enter the room.

At 10 am, following the order to rise by the judge, we all stood up. A while after, the president and vice president entered the courtroom. The president looked a little thinner but I was somewhat relieved when I saw his well-groomed hair and a fresher-looking prison uniform. Each time when President Kim answered to questions, I felt sad and depressed. Why does he have to be so tense? I prayed silently, 'Oh Lord, please help him! Give him wisdom!'

Thanks to the defense lawyer's focused arguments, I relaxed gradually. I felt more comfortable when the prosecutor stated that there was nothing more to ask. The moment when the president and the vice president rose and turned around, everyone stood up spontaneously all of sudden. Certainly, no one was waiting for someone else to get up first. No one was ordering us to stand up. People's spontaneous action came naturally from their feeling of respect! So, we all stood up twice! Once to the order of the judge and the other for the spontaneous standing for respect. Even now my eyes get wet when I think about it. I cannot fully describe the prosecutor and the court staff's bewildered expressions when everyone exited the courtroom so quietly and orderly. We lined up along the path where the vehicle transporting the president and vice president passed, and although the dark smoke-colored vehicle window prevented us from seeing inside, we all waved our hands to show that we were standing behind them. President Kim! Vice President Oh! We love you!

A Feast amidst Adversity

All the parents, students, and professors gathered at a church, which was about 10 minutes from the courthouse, whenever there was a trial. Parents in Daegu always prepared lunches for the hundreds of Handong family visiting to see the trial.

That day, the church cafeteria looked like a feast. Daegu parents in aprons distributed piles of food to visitors who came from all over the country, and said excitedly, "When we think about how hard it must be for President Kim and Vice President Oh inside that prison, this is nothing. Now that they can come out of the prison to partici-pate in the trial, we are so happy we could dance."

Seeing their excitement, attorney Lee commented, "Handong is a very strange school. This is evident when I look at President Kim. It's strange that a world-famous scientist is suffering like this. It's strange that Dr. Y. Lee, who had been the prime minister of our country, has become the Chairman of Handong, which is going through so much hardship and adversity. It's also strange that Pastor Ha faithfully helps the school despite all the hardships that the school has caused him. It's strange that I, an attorney who has been busily working in Seoul for the last 20 years, am now the attorney for Handong in Pohang. The even more incomprehensible ones are the parents. All the people who cannot be understood with regular reasoning must have gathered here. I have never heard of such a thing as a parents' prayer circle at other universities in Korea. You are not parents of kindergarten children, and yet I hear that some of you woke up at 4 o'clock this morning to come to Daegu and see the trial in person. This cannot be understood with an ordinary logic. I thank God that I can join you who are beyond common sense.

"When I look at the course of Handong's legal battles, I notice that no judge who started the trial stayed with the trial until it ended. For five years, every time there was a change in the presiding judge, we had a new, fair judge who ruled in our favor. That is because God was with us. In this case too, God will be our judge. Since all of you parents are praying so hard for this trial, I do not worry. Please continue to pray for us."

Even in the midst of such circumstances, the parents were deep in joyful conversations. One mother joked how her husband, who drove her to the carpool in Seoul early in the morning every time there was a trial, asked, "Will Handong not graduate your son if you don't go down there this early in the morning?" Someone joined and said, "When we are old and our memory becomes poor, we will all forget our own alma maters and ask each other, 'What class of Handong were we?' 'Who was our advisor?' 'Oh yes, it was the white-haired Professor Young-Gil Kim!'" We all laughed.

"The Maker of heaven and earth, the sea, and everything in them – the Lord, who remains faithful forever. He upholds the cause of the oppressed and gives food to the hungry. The Lord sets prisoners free" (Psalm 146:6-7).

The round trip from Seoul to Daegu took 10 hours. But those hours were filled with passionate testimonies. Because the parents were so eager to talk about how they were led to send their children to Handong or how their children had been transformed after attending Handong, they instituted a fine of $10 whenever someone talked for more than five minutes. They said that even these "fines" made them happy because they could collect more funds for the school, since everyone ended up having to pay the fine any way.

When the Prison Doors Opened

On July 4, 2001, as the heat of early summer began, Young-Gil and Vice President Oh were released on bail after an imprisonment of 54 days. *"Then they cried to the Lord in their trouble, and he saved them from their distress. He brought them out of darkness and the deepest gloom and broke away their chains. Let them give thanks to the Lord for his unfailing love and his wonderful deeds for men, for he breaks down gates of bronze and cuts through bars of iron" (Psalm 107:13-16).*

My hands shook as I gathered Young-Gil's suit. It was a completely different feeling than the day before when I made a trip to visit him. I finally saw the beautiful greens of early summer. The entrance to the prison was crowded with happy faces for a change. Students, parents, and professors came with welcome placards and were anxiously waiting for Young-Gil and Vice President Oh to appear. They took longer than we had expected, but at last when they came out, big bursts of cheers covered the grounds.

As they greeted each person who had come to see them, a few prison guards who had been watching began to shed tears. They approached me with great emotion on their faces and said, "Mrs. Kim, you have been through so much, but we have spent precious moments in here with President Kim and Vice President Oh. After spending decades as prison guards, we came to have hope from the fact that there are people like them in our country."

The following note was posted on Handong's website by a student who was present when the prison doors opened:

When I was at the student body office, I heard that the president and the vice president would be released on bail. I hurriedly headed for the Daegu Prison along with a number of professors. While I was waiting with a score of parents and professors in front of the prison gate from which our leaders would walk out, the various incidents that had taken place and the hardship that they must have endured passed through my head.

After the announcement that they would be released at 3 pm, the gate opened and I saw them. The president was wearing a thick black-horn frame eyeglasses and a black suit. The president silently hugged each person with tears in his eyes, and some professors cried like a child. The prison guards also sobbed saying how blessed they were through their time with the president. The president and vice president then left for Sunlin Good Samaritan Hospital for health check up.

Today was truly a happy day as I could see the president once again waving his hands with his child-like smile. Although the case is not yet terminated, let's all pray that they recover their health quickly and regain peace of mind to concentrate on school affairs again.

CHAPTER 12:

For Surely I Will Deliver You

God is Watching

On the day of their release, Young-Gil went directly to the Sunlin Good Samaritan Hospital for a medical examination. Young-Gil joked as he entered the hospital room, "Hey, there are no steel bars on the windows!"

When the dermatologist came in, he said to me, "Why don't you wait outside?"

I wondered what it was about, but I had to leave the room. Because I was curious, I peeked inside the room. At that moment, I could see Young-Gil's buttocks, where the skin had festered and become swollen, with red ulcers and open sores. After the doctor dressed the area, I went inside and asked in shock, "Young-Gil, what happened?"

"I told you to go out because I didn't want you to see. It's nothing. Prison rules tell us to always sit up straight with our legs crossed. So I always sat in one position from morning to night, and some infection developed into sores on the area due to heat rash."

"My goodness! You sat all day long while this was happening? No one would've been watching you since you were in a private cell in Daegu prison. Why didn't you stretch your legs, or sit in different positions?"

When I replied in resentment, Young-Gil looked at me as if he could not understand me and said, "No! You shouldn't do that! If they tell you to sit up straight, then you should sit up straight! How can you not obey the prison's rules? Even if men are not watching, God is watching."

Right after he finished his examinations at the hospital, he ran back to school as if nothing had happened and busily took care of all the work that had piled up. For the first time in a long while, I went home and wept on my knees. I was overwhelmed with joy and shed tears of thanksgiving for the indescribable love and guidance of our God the Father.

The Hand That Holds the Stick

In early June 2001, when Young-Gil was still in Daegu Prison, elder H.Lee, the Chairman of the Korean Elders Association visited him. He had a sharp but gentle face, and he extended a surprising invitation to Young-Gil while he was in prison.

"President Kim, we'd like to invite you to be the main speaker at our annual national meeting of elders next month on July 24, 2001"

"Elder Lee, I'm in prison, and I'm not sure when I'll be able to leave."

"We all believe that you will be out of prison by then. All the elders across the country are praying for Handong and you."

"If I'm out by that time, then I'll obey."

When the elder came out of the visiting room, he also encouraged me.

"Mrs. Kim, this incident has taken place in the will of God, so do not worry about anything, but instead, give thanks to God. God chose and called President Kim and then humbled him, so it will be God who will raise him up again. There are always amazing blessings from God awaiting us after a time of hardship. Because of a layman scientist, an educator and an elder who has been persecuted and sent to prison, 120,000 elders across the country are now praying with one heart.

"If anything goes wrong, then the churches of Korea will be reprimanded by God. Let's wait in patience until God decides to act. Those who sent President Kim to prison are actually the stick that

God is using to refine President Kim. Do not resent the stick. Look at the hand that is holding the stick. Whose hand do you think that is?"

God used this man, whom we had not met before, as His messenger, and He gave us new comfort and a mission through him.

God set Young-Gil free in time to honor the invitation extended by Elder Lee. Finally, on the day when we traveled to speak before the group of elders, Young-Gil closed his eyes and sang a hymn.

Thou, my everlasting portion
More than friend or life to me
All along my pilgrim journey
Savior, let me walk with Thee

Not for ease or worldly pleasure
Nor for fame my prayer shall be
Gladly will I toil and suffer
Only let me walk with thee

Lead me thro' the vale of shadows
Bear me o'er life's fitful sea
Then the gate of life eternal
May I enter, Lord, with Thee

Close to Thee, close to Thee
Close to Thee, close to Thee
All along my pilgrim journey
Savior, let me walk with Thee
(F. J. Crosby, 1820-1915)

The hotel was packed with elders from all over the country. Elder Lee gave the opening remarks.

"We almost missed out on hearing Elder Young-Gil Kim's lecture here at our twenty-seventh meeting, but we thank God that His grace has allowed us to hear his testimony in person."

Young-Gil, however, did not speak about his experience in prison. He spoke about Jesus Christ.

"I'd like to sing a hymn to end my testimony. Our Lord said, *"Whoever comes to me I will never drive away" (John 6:37).* **"He now showed them** *the full extent of his love" (John 13:1).* The hymn that says 'If Thou withdraw Thyself from me, Ah! Whither shall I go?' does not correctly portray the heart of God. I'd like to sing a revised version of the hymn that I sang a lot when I was in prison."

Father I stretch my hands to Thee
No other help I know
Thou loves me so
And I thank Thee

What did Thine only Son endure
Before I drew my breath!
What pain, what labour, to secure
My soul from endless death!

O Spirit, could I this believe
I now should feel Thy power
And all my wants Thou wouldst relieve
In this accepted hour

I do believe, I now believe
That Jesus died for me
And that He shed His precious blood
From sin to set me free
Slightly revised, (C. Wesley, 1741)

The Price of President for a Day

While Young-Gil and the Vice President Oh were in prison, students voluntarily began to collect legal defence funds. Various musical groups on campus hosted fund-raising concerts. *"Sing to the Lord! Give praise to the Lord! He rescues the life of the needy from the hands of the wicked" (Jeremiah 20:13).*

Students who had won art competitions in the architectural design division donated all of their award money.

"When we first saw the announcement for the competition, we felt that we need to win so that we could support the legal defence funds for President Kim and Vice President Oh. We prayed every day as we prepared our works and submitted them with trembling hearts."

Along with the donation from churches, friends, and sponsoring members, HGU received about $4.6 million in donations during the 53 days of Young-Gil and Vice President Oh's imprisonment. One professor joked, "I calculated the price for a day's worth of your imprisonment, and it came out to be $80,000 a day. I know it was difficult for you two, but thinking of the school, perhaps, you should have stayed there a little longer!"

Do not let Your Right Hand Know What Your Left Hand has Done

Thanks to donations from many supporters, funds for our legal expenses continued to increase. Encouragement, love and support came from across the country as well as worldwide. Were we really qualified to receive all these undeserved acts of kindness and love? Young-Gil was certainly a man of many blessings, from the beginning to the end. As his wife, I was always trailing behind him, becoming disappointed and fearful at times, but I too was often moved by his pure passion for faith, tasting the joy amidst hardship.

"Mrs. Kim, do you know someone named Ms. J. Lee? She donated $170,000. I wonder who would send this large a sum without any notice." The finance manager said one day with great curiosity, as if unable to solve a mystery.

"I don't know her. Have you asked Young-Gil?"

Young-Gil said that the name was also unfamiliar to him. Later that day, the finance manager said, "I finally found her phone number by contacting the bank. I asked her to meet me, but she resolutely refused."

So, I called her.

"I go to the same church as you do. God told me to send that money to Handong, and I've merely run His errand."

"Since you sent this large a sum of money, there must be a testimony that you need to share with us. That's how God will be glorified. Please meet with me."

She finally gave in and agreed to meet us after service on the following Sunday.

After the worship service, we kept turning our heads in all directions. We wanted her to recognize us and find us. As we greeted people who came up to us to say hello, we continued to look around to see if one of them might be her. Then, a tall, well-groomed woman approached us. It was Ms. J. Lee.

"Ms. Lee, we'd like to treat you lunch, I said after the greeting."

"I don't eat expensive food. I'm happy with just a bowl of noodles."

As we sat together at a restaurant near the church, she told us her story.

"During my sophomore year in college, when I was wandering aimlessly without any purpose for my life, I accepted Jesus Christ as my Lord and Savior. From then on, my life changed from darkness to light. God has not yet allowed a spouse for me, so I live alone."

She appeared to be in her late forties. She possessed spiritual dignity, and her devotion to the Lord radiated a certain beauty.

"I don't own have much. All my wealth only amounted to a small pharmacy, and it has been sold recently. I decided long ago to use it for God's kingdom. To my surprise, God told me to send not only all the proceeds from the pharmacy, but my savings as well, to Handong Global University. I've only obeyed God's command."

She was still uncomfortable that her deed had become known. She said, "The Lord told us to not let our right hand know what our left hand is doing. How can this be possible? To me, these words say that we should not only act without others knowing, but even without ourselves knowing, that we should forget even our own memories. So, please don't thank me. Just thank God who gave me that command."

The impression from that meeting still remain in my memories like the subtle aroma of flowers, knowing that the source of the aroma comes from Jesus Christ, whom she cherished in her heart as her treasure!

Intercessors for Handong in Bangkok

In January 2002, when we were visiting Bangkok, Thailand, one of the parents of Handong students invited us to a famous local restaurant. As we were about to sit down, one of the parents looked toward the entrance and exclaimed in a shocked voice, "There comes someone whom you must meet before leaving!"

He pointed to a woman coming into the restaurant with five or six other guests.

"When you were in prison, she visited all the Korean churches in Bangkok and asked them to sign a petition requesting your release."

A beautiful middle-aged woman approached us. She was overwhelmed with surprise and joy by the unexpected encounter, and she said to us with tears in her eyes, "I can't believe I'm seeing you in person now when I'd only seen your pictures in the newspapers and on websites till now! God, thank you! I've been living in Bangkok for 20 years, and I'd always missed my home country. And so I had been even more interested in Handong Global University. Whenever I heard negative news from Korea, I always thought that Handong was the future of our country. Then, one day, when I heard about your arrest, I did not know what to do. I assumed that it was misinformation and went to the Handong website. From that day on, my daily schedule after work was to run to my computer. It was just as I had expected. Reading all the petitions, newspaper articles, and encouragement letters, I cried at my desk every day. I thought that, perhaps, a petition signed by Koreans living in Bangkok might help."

There were Handong supporters even in this city! Of all the restaurants in Bangkok, how amazing that we would run into her in this place at this time! It was as if God had the world map in front of Him and was looking for Handong intercessors from all corners of the world. *"I am a friend to all who fear you, to all who follow your precepts" (Psalm 119:63).* Two years later, her son transferred to Handong from a Thai university.

For Surely I Will Deliver You

On December 28, 2001, the appeal trial at the Daegu Appellate Court 41 was to open at 10 am in the morning. The trial that had begun in early spring continued through the dead heat of summer, and was to end in the winter. Handong parents, students, and professors, as well as the local media, gathered outside to hear the final verdict, waiting for the court session to begin. Everyone looked anxious, wondering what the final verdict would be. It was a sunny day, but a bitter gusty wind was blowing through the court grounds as if wanting to sweep away all our past trials and hardships.

Young-Gil had stood before the court countless times, but I could never sit inside. Because of my trembling and fearful heart, I usually stayed in the car or walked around the courthouse, praying silently to the Father in heaven. That day as well, I stood outside the courthouse in the gusty wind, praying for the trial to end. *"But I will rescue you on that day, declares the Lord; you will not be handed over to those you fear. I will save you; you will not fall by the sword but will escape with your life, because you trust in me, declares the Lord" (Jeremiah 39:17-18).*

Time passed, and people began to exit the courthouse, unable to hide their joy. They told me that as soon as our case number was called, the judge took only about ten minutes to read his verdict. On major offenses, the judge declared "not guilty," and for a few minor offenses, assessed a fine.

The media all reported on this verdict: "After the first trial, the current President and Vice President were arrested in the court but later released on bail. The eyes and ears of the country had been focused on the appeal, and the appellate court overturned the lower court's decisions again drawing great interest across the country."

During an interview, the Chairman of the Parents Association said, "I'm overjoyed. We all prayed that we would get a verdict that would not interfere with President Kim doing his job. God has answered our prayers. The justice that was long over-due was finally recovered."

Attorney Lee said, "Who would gain by turning a civil suit into a criminal one, and by attacking an old issue? A wrong verdict has raised public criticism across the country and hurt our students – no one has gained from all of this. Today's decision by the appellate court shows that it is wrong to criminalize small administrative mistakes that occurred while managing a school."

Lawyer's Timetable and God's Timetable

In April, 2003, Attorney J. Lee donated to Handong more than 1,000 volumes books that he collected throughout his life time. At a chapel service, he gave his testimony to the students:

"Born as a Christian in a Christian family, I used to go to church like a visitor, only to attend worship services. Because I was often harassed day and night by endless phone calls from the church people asking for legal advices, I moved to another church. I wanted to escape from the people and phone calls, but I guess I could not hide from God. It was from the new church that I got involved in Handong's case.

"One day, not long after I joined the new church, I learnt that Pastor Ha, the then chairman of the board, and President Young-Gil Kim were sued for violation of a private school law. I felt a sense of mission to help them out since both of them were relatively ignorant of worldly affairs.

"Initially, the case didn't look too complicated. Since I was aware that the school did not have the money to defend itself, I volunteered to work for them free of charge. I thought this would be an easy way to show off my good deeds, and I simply thought that, perhaps, after 5 to 6 trips to Pohang, it would be over.

"The civil suit that I figured would end quickly, however, soon developed into a major criminal litigation and resulted in arresting and physical detention of President Kim and Vice President Oh. The volunteer service that I started casually, came to determine the very existence of Handong. If we lose, Handong would turn into an ordinary city university, and Pastor Ha, President Kim and the entire directors of the board would be replaced.

"After over 40 trips between Seoul and Pohang, and 7 years of toil, we finally won the case in January 2002. If it were not for the prayers of Handong's family, pastors in Christian circle and 20,000 or so Handong sponsors, today's Handong would not be around. God showed the world that He is behind us and that Handong is undoubtedly His school. Nobody expected that a school that could not even pay its staff wages would win in the litigation against the plaintiff who tried to exercise economic and political influence to take over the school. I just heard the good news that our efforts to reconcile with the opposition group have finally been successful. While winning the court case was a victory, reconciliation is a true victory that comes from God.

"While serving Handong, I realize that there aren't that many people who were as blessed as I was. The time and money I dedicated to God to help defend Handong is richly rewarded by God. He made my law firm successful in many other difficult cases where our chance of winning seemed slim.

"I had often complained to God for his slow response. Through my experience with Handong, however, I came to see clearly that God's timetable is different from the attorney's timetable. Dear students, if you encounter a case where a response from God is slow, please wait patiently. I am now very happy to donate to Handong School of Law some 1,000 volumes of court case records that I have collected while serving as a lawyer for the past 37 years."

Our suffering was exposed to the world, and the hardship of Handong was no longer ours alone. Henri Nouwen once sang of God, who turns our mourning into dancing (Psalm 30:11). God molds us through trials. Trials are the very place where God calls us to take our first steps and dance with Him.

This dance does not happen by chance. In order to take that first step, we need the practice that comes through trials and following the path unseen. There is no growth without pain, and glory is hidden in trials and suffering. In the midst of pain, God taught me that He Himself is my only shield and my very great reward (Genesis 15:1), and He made me see areas where I needed healing. God wove all my sorrows and joys into one and made me take my steps in adoration and joy.

The place of trials was a place where we no longer remained in our sorrows but instead held His hand to move to a place of dancing with more freedom. Our gracious God does not take us to a place insulated from pain, but instead He uses our pain and loss to prepare us for a greater purpose within His plan – because we discover God's grace in the midst of sorrows.

Another Weapon within God's Plan

On October 16, 2003, we won in the Supreme Court. Attorney Lee told us that this verdict was a 120% victory for the school. God made us pray up to the very last moment so that we would not become proud! It was a dramatic reversal by God.

"In the Lord I take refuge. How then can you say to me: 'Flee like a bird to your mountain. For look, the wicked bend their bows; they set their arrows against the string to shoot from the shadows at the upright in heart. When the foundations are being destroyed, what can the righteous do?' The Lord is in his holy temple; the Lord is on his heavenly throne. He observes the sons of men; his eyes examine them" (Psalm 11:1-4).

In "A Tale of Three Kings," Gene Edwards says that God uses even unjust weapons to accomplish His will: "Why are there so few students enrolled at the school that teaches obedience and broken-ness? That's because of the many trials that students at this school must suffer through. It's because of the unbroken leaders who cause suffering. They are the unbroken authority that God has chosen with sovereignty." Those who had opposed Handong becoming a Christian university were just another weapon that God had anointed for his purpose.

Because I Trust 'My Bondage'

In March 2001, President Gaylen Byker of Calvin College in Grand Rapids, Michigan visited HGU while touring several Korean Christian universities. After he returned to the United States, he sent Professor Elizabeth Vander Lei to pursue a sister-school rela-tionship between Calvin and Handong. President Byker said that he was impressed by Handong students' ability to understand his lectures in English and the school's refreshing Christian environ-ment. Unfortunately, Professor Vander Lei arrived at Handong few days after the arrest of Young-Gil and the Vice President.

Professor Vander Lei did not know what to do in light of such shocking news. She was not sure what Young-Gil had done wrong, but how could such a thing happen to a university with which her school was about form a sister relationship? Later, she

admitted that she did not know what to report to her university president about a school

whose president had been imprisoned. She stayed at the school for several days, and during that period, she was moved as she saw Handong's professors and students gather at the chapel several times a day to pray in tears for their president and vice president. Gradually she came to understand what really had happened, and wrote a lengthy report

to President Byker recording all that she saw and felt.

I have heard later that Calvin College seriously discussed the issue, and some of the professors stated that "it would be better to pursue a sister relationship with Handong once its legal problems have been resolved and its president has been released from prison." But, President Byker responded firmly, "Did Paul and Joseph go to prison because they had committed a crime? Even in our times, people of faith will be persecuted when they do the work of God. Our college must not delay in working with Handong, which is under persecution today."

Acts of the Holy Spirit is being written today at Handong. I thank God that we have established a sister-school relationship with such a university.

From then on, Calvin College has been one of the most active sister schools, one that understands Handong better than any other.

PART IV: MISSION

CHAPTER 13:

Kernels of A Wheat Scattered In Fiji

Why God?

Students who completed one semester of a program called the Handong Discipleship School(HDS) participate in short-term missions to overseas during breaks. In early July 1997, many mission teams traveled with professors to China, Indonesia, Sri Lanka, Uzbekistan, and Fiji ,among others.

On July 10, 1997, Professor Y. Kim called from Fiji, where he had taken a team of students on a mission trip. A missionary, Pastor J. Kim, who was the principal of Vision College, a technical training school in Fiji, had invited 10 Handong students to teach computer skills to the Polynesians. Most of the people in Fiji are Polynesians or ethnic Indians and Chinese who followed Islam or Hinduism.

Five days after the team departed for Fiji, I received an urgent phone call from Professor Y. Kim.

"Mrs. Kim, where is President Kim?"

His tense voice told me that something was wrong. I asked cautiously, "He's at the school. What's wrong?"

"We had an accident. One of the Handong students, Kyung-Sik, was swept up by the waves and has drowned, and the other student Young-Min is missing."

His lifeless voice hit my ears like a bolt of lightning. I collapsed on the floor, still holding the handset. I barely maintained consciousness as I tried to listen to what he was saying.

"Water is precious here, so five male students dug a pond in a corner of the school grounds to trap the rain water coming down from the mountains. Then they walked over to the ocean across from the school. They said that the ocean was calm and peaceful with no wind. The students went as far as the breakwater surrounded by coral reefs, and suddenly a huge wave struck them and washed the two of them away in an instant. Only the body of Kyung-Sik was found."

Kyung-Sik Kang and Young-Min Kwon were both members of the charter class at Handong. They had helped with school during its difficulties without going home for breaks.

"God, why did You let this happen? How can we deliver such news to their parents?"

I felt devastated, as if the sky had fallen. A light rain was sprinkling outside. As I was sitting with no way to sort through my thoughts, someone said to me, "Mrs. Kim, God's providence must have been at work. Let us pray that the parents can successfully endure this pain."

After coming up with an emergency plan, two professors left for Daegu city where Young-Min's parents lived, and another two professors for Daejon city where Kyung-Sik's parents lived. How heavy their footsteps must have been as they traveled to tell the news of the loss! A memorial service for Kyung-Sik was set up at school. Students who had gone home for the break heard of the tragic news and returned to school one by one. They knelt in front of Kyung-Sik's picture, which was adorned with a black ribbon, and shed endless tears. It was the worst tragedy since our school had opened. Rain covered the campus with indifference. That evening, the professors who had left for Daegu and Daejon cities called.

"The parents collapsed from the terrible shock of such news, but they were courageous and resolute. Amidst such a crisis, they were worried for the school."

The parents and staff prepared to leave for Fiji. The waiting area at the airport that day was full of sorrow. Friends who had gathered just a few days before to send them off with encouragement were now gathering for a farewell to heaven. Kyung-Sik's mother said, "Kyung-Sik always wanted to become a missionary. I sincerely thank all the Handong professors for teaching and guiding Kyung-Sik so well until now."

At a loss for words, I held onto her hands. A while later, Young-Min's parents arrived. I could not bring myself to look at his mother, whose lips were swollen with blisters. Young-Min's mother said, "God raises and calms the waves, and He knows all the inner workings of the ocean. If He wanted to bring Young-Min to life, He would save him just as He did Jonah. I have taught about heaven and resurrection to my son, so how can I despair like an unbeliever now?"

They did not resent us or blame the school. Instead, they encouraged Professor Kim's wife, who was standing in a corner by herself, consumed by sorrow and anguish.

Oaks of Righteousness, a Planting of the Lord

Two days later, Young-Gil and I departed for Fiji. That morning in his study, he wailed with insurmountable grief.

"God, I could bear all kinds of difficulties during these last few years, but this tragedy is too much to bear. Tell me your reasons for taking away our students!"

Sometime later, he walked out of his study with tears on his face and said, "God gave me Isaiah 61:3. *"Provide for those who grieve in Zion – to bestow on them a crown of beauty instead of ashes, the oil of gladness instead of mourning, and a garment of praise instead of a spirit of despair. They will be called oaks of righteousness, a planting of the Lord for the display of his splendor."* God's calling for Kyung-Sik and Young-Min is of great pain and loss to those of us who are living on this earth, but they will glorify God as they become 'oaks of righteousness' that God has planted!"

Going through the airport counters with two urns in his hands, he wiped his endless tears with his shirtsleeve.

We arrived in Fiji and drove for several hours toward Vision College near the coast. The school consisted of only two classrooms; it reminded us of the simple schoolhouses in rural Korea. The culprit ocean across from the school was peaceful and silent as if nothing had happened, reflecting the indigo sky of the South Pacific. Many people, including local government officials, the chief of the local village, local residents from the village as well as neighboring towns, staff from the Korean embassy, missionaries, and the rest of the Handong students, had gathered on the school grounds, waiting for our arrival. Everyone was mournfully silent.

Not knowing if Young-Min was dead or alive, we conducted a "Farewell to Heaven" memorial service for Kyung-Sik. Underneath the banner that read "Farewell Service to Heaven for Kyung-Sik" sat a coffin holding Kyung-Sik's body, decked in nameless flowers.

**Farewell Service to Heaven for the first missionary
student in Fiji on July12, 1997**

The extreme heat of the tropical sun beat down on our heads. Standing on the desolate school grounds, the students of Vision College, wearing traditional Polynesian clothes, sang a hymn in Korean.

Rock of Ages, cleft for me
Let me hide myself in Thee
Let the water and the blood
From Thy wounded side which flowed

Be of sin the double cure
Cleanse me from its guilt and power.
(A.M. Toplady, 1776)

When Kyung-Sik's mother delivered her final good-bye to her son, she covered her mouth and cried.

"Kyung-Sik was molded from dust, and I can only thank God for allowing him to return to dust in this clean, uncontaminated land. President Kim! Kyung-Sik was the first member of the first class of students at Handong, and God has received him as the first fruit of Handong's martyrdom. Can we call this coincidence? On the morning of his departure for Fiji, he bowed deeply as if leaving on a long trip and said, 'Father, mother, thank you for raising me with such love.' Kyung-Sik matured a lot at Handong. I thank the school for preparing him, and it is an honor for my family that God has accepted our son as his pleasing sacrifice. Kyung-Sik, the saxophone that you wanted so much – you can now ask your Father in heaven for one there. Practice a lot, and let us hear it when we meet again in heaven."

Even if You do not do as we Hope

The search operation for Young-Min continued for several days with the help of the Fiji naval police. Young-Min's father never gave up hope that his son might be alive, and he accompanied the search team every day. We desperately hoped that Young-Min would come back to us alive, but as the days passed, hope dimmed. It was heart-wrenching to watch Kyung-Sik's parents, who had at least found their son's body, consoling the parents of Young-Min. I prayed, "God You saved Jonah from the depth of the ocean, even from the belly of a giant fish. Please find Young-Min for us!"

God's voice came to me in my mourning.

"Woman, why are you crying?" (John 20:13). "Why do you look for the living among the dead?" (Luke 24:5).

God was comforting us with the words that the angels had spoken to Mary Magdalene when she was in tears for not being able to find the body of Jesus.

"Why are you crying? Why do you look for Young-Min in the ocean when he is with Me? Young-Min is now with Me in My house. So do not weep anymore."

"Jesus said to her, 'I am the resurrection and the life. He who believes in me will live, even though he dies; and whoever lives and believes in me will never die. Do you believe this?" (John 11:25-26).

Did they know that they were going to be offered as sacrifices of martyrdom on this earth? Were they preparing themselves to be offered to our Lord as fragrant sacrifices before their youths had withered? We discovered a quote by the famous Pastor K.C. Choo in Young-Min's diary. Pastor Choo had been a defining person of Korean Christian history. He lived during the era of Japan's occupation of Korea (1910-1945), and he was imprisoned and tortured for six years for refusing to participate in Japanese shrine worship. He was martyred in 1945.

"The pine tree is most green before it dies, and the lily is most fragrant when it falls before it withers. John the Baptist at the age of 31, and Stephen as a young man, both shed their blood in their prime. This body too will become a sacrifice for the Lord before it withers."

That evening, the parents of the two students sang a hymn together.

> I'd rather have Jesus than silver or gold
> I'd rather be His than have riches untold
> I'd rather have Jesus than houses or lands
> I'd rather be led by His nail-pierced hand
> Than to be the king of a vast domain
> Or be held in sin's dread sway
> I'd rather have Jesus than anything
> This world affords today
> (R. F. Miller, 1925)

Extreme grief had turned into the oil of joy, and sorrow was clothed with praise. The day we left Fiji without having found Young-Min's body, his father said, "My heart was in hell when I arrived here, but now I leave having tasted heaven. Seeing the lives of missionaries here who gave up their comfortable lives in their home countries, I leave having discovered a new world."

The message at Young-Min's memorial service brought comfort to us all.

"About 40 years ago, Jim Elliott and five friends who were students at Wheaton College left to preach the Gospel in Ecuador. On the day they arrived, they were killed by the natives without ever uttering a word about the Gospel. Even American missionary groups thought their actions were rash.

But one year later, when Jim's wife Elizabeth Elliott followed in her husband's footsteps and visited Ecuador, the doors to the Gospel finally began to open. Seeing her who had sought out Ecuador even though her husband had been killed there, the natives slowly began to understand that her love was real. The event sparked a spiritual revival at Wheaton College, and it became a great school blessed by God. I am confident that God's glory and blessings will be with Handong, which has sacrificed its first martyr."

Just as the pastor had said, a few months later, we received news that about 700 Fijian natives had accepted Jesus Christ as their Savior. Young-Min and Kyung-Sik were the sacrifices of martyrdom that God had accepted, and the 700 Fijians were their first fruits. *"I tell you the truth, unless a kernel of wheat falls to the ground and dies, it remains only a single seed. But if it dies, it produces many seeds"* (*John 12:24).* In these times of few martyrs, Onnuri Presbyterian Church built "Handong Hall" in honor of Kyung-Sik and Young-Min.

After we returned from Fiji, we received a letter from a student that encouraged our hearts.

Dear President Kim!

Today during the memorial service for Young-Min, I saw the tears that flowed down your face. I cried too, but my tears were not only the tears of sadness over the loss of Kyung-Sik and Young-Min. In this small school, the two brothers' martyrdom is most certainly not an ordinary sacrifice.

When you spoke the words 'they who had come from a barren land of nothingness with only God as their focus...' and cried without being able to continue, why was I so sad? Why did such a tragedy fall upon us when we had come to this place with only the name of Jesus as our guide? However, I thank the Lord who has answered you with the words of Isaiah 61:3.

On this summer day of blue skies and green grass, I am happy despite this sadness. It is because I have a vision and a dream that God has given me. I believe that the vision of Handong students will only become clearer and stronger because of this incident. Our two brothers will be praying for us Handong students from heaven, and I know that the angels will be lifting us up.

Our beloved President Kim, push us even harder. Pray for us that we may be able to sacrifice even more for God's university. We need you, President Kim. We love your smiles and your familiar accent. We love hearing your voice as you pat our shoulders in the cafeteria asking, 'Did you have lunch?'

Seeing you today, a photograph I had seen in a magazine came to mind. It was your picture in which you were looking out at a vast expanse of yellow earth. In 1995, as the school prepared to open its doors, what were you thinking about when you saw the empty land of our campus? Was it worry, anxiety, apprehension? Or, was it hope, aspiration, and the glory of God? I am certain that Handong will reveal God's justice and glory, and spread the Gospel throughout the earth! And for this, I believe that God has raised you as our captain to serve in this amazing history of our Lord, and that God has called us as His disciples who need training, encouragement, and confidence from you! President Kim! Do not mourn any longer. Look at us. We are mere children, but expect big things as we mature.

"But you, keep your head in all situations, endure hardship, do the work of an evangelist, discharge all the duties of your ministry.

For I am already being poured out like a drink offering, and the time has come for my departure. I have fought the good fight, I have finished the race, I have kept the faith. Now there is in store for me the crown of righteousness, which the Lord, the righteous Judge, will award to me on that day – and not only to me, but also to all who have longed for his appearing" (II Timothy 4:5-8).

God is Anxious!

"Mrs. Kim, God is anxious when He sees me!"

It was Young-Min's mother on the phone.

"What? God is anxious?" I was puzzled.

"I've cried a lot – whenever I see Young-Min's belongings, or when I see the back of a tall young man on the streets. I wish for a sight of him even in my dreams, to be able to hear his voice just once. Whenever I miss him, I become sleepy as if I've been anesthetized, regardless of the time of day or how much sleep I've had. After a short nap, I feel peace again in my heart. I think God is flustered whenever I'm about to cry. I feel like He is following me around with a shot of anesthesia, and He puts me into a short sleep and says, 'My daughter, I get concerned whenever you seem so sad. My dear daughter, do not cry. Young-Min is with Me in happiness."

Listening to Young-Min's mother's story, I covered the handset mouthpiece with one hand and cried in silence too. 'Lord, death is too sad for us living on this earth.'

Those of us who live on this earth lose our loved ones and cry out in futile sorrow and agony. The same Jesus, who saw the death of Lazarus and wept, is now shedding tears by our side as He sees our grief. *"When Jesus saw her weeping, and the Jews who had come along with her also weeping, he was deeply moved in spirit and troubled. 'Where have you laid him?' he asked. 'Come and see, Lord,' they replied. Jesus wept" (John 11:33-35).*

Kyung-Sik's mother and Young-Min's mother, like Daniel, faithfully trusted God, who oversees life and death, fortune and misfortune, even though He did not do as they had hoped for and did not bring their sons back to life. They never lost their peace of mind. *"You will keep in perfect peace him whose mind is steadfast, because he trusts in you" (Isaiah 26:3).*

CHAPTER 14:

Enlarge the Site of Your Tent

Reaching out to help the World

The world in the 21st century is undergoing rapid globalization - politically, economically, culturally, and socially. Dizzying technological advancements in information technology, communication technology, and the Internet fuel this phenomenon. Young-Gil says that Handong's vision is to build a global network of the future leaders who will work together to achieve global prosperity and peace in the 21st century. How can Handong's graduates be effective leaders to serve and change this world? They must be educated and trained to think not only critically but also multi-culturally in solving complex problems of this technology-driven, globalizing world. They must have the capacity and innovativeness to think beyond the national borders. They must be fluent in as many major languages as possible. They must know how to rapidly adapt to changes. They must be open to the challenges different cultures present to them.

Every year, more and more students from North and Central Asia, Southeast Asia, Africa, Eastern Europe, and Central & Latin America come to study at Handong. So far, students from some fifty eight countries studied at Handing. Certain major fields in undergraduate program are taught in English. Handong started a joint MBA program with the Institute of Finance and Economics (IFE) in Ulaanbaatar, Mongolia, in 1999. As of 2005, some 50 Mongolian graduates from this joint program are working for Mongolian government agencies, multinational companies, bank, and universities. We feel rewarded when we receive positive feedbacks from our graduates who say that the program has helped them work more effectively. From 2006, this joint program will be co-sponsored by UNESCO as a part of the UNITWIN/UNESCO program.

In September 2003, Handong concluded an agreement with the Ministry of Higher and Secondary Specialized Education of Uzbekistan and Tashkent State University of Economics to establish joint MBA program. In August 2005, HGU agreed to conduct training program for young Uzbek teachers in cooperation with the government of Uzbekistan. The program will encourage the participants to acquire practical and updated pedagogical skills to bring out talents endowed in their students.

Our cooperation with developing countries also includes Afghanistan. In April 2003, HGU made an agreement with the Afghan Ministry of Higher Education and Khandahar University to support their development efforts. Using summer vacations, Handong professors and students go to Afghanistan to teach IT, business, and industrial design at Khandahar University.

As I witness the various international cooperation that are taking place, I see how God uses Handong to spread His love around the globe.

"And how can they preach unless they are sent? As it is written, 'How beautiful are the feet of those who bring good news!'" (Romans 10:15).

A Dream for International Law School Realized

Young-Gil had several God-given visions, one of them being a dream to establish Handong International Law School (HILS). He began to share his dream with others, and talked about the need for Korea as well as other developing countries to produce international lawyers to expand their markets in the global community. Since Korea joined the Organization for Economic Cooperation and Development (OECD), Korea's legal market will open to the world and legal issues involving international parties will grow. Korea is receiving an ever-increasing demand for professionals in the fields of international law and trades, yet there is a dire shortage of international legal professionals in Korea now. One must establish an international law school based on the U.S. law-school system and cultivate international law professionals who can work on the global stage.

In October 2000, U. S. attorney S. K. Lee from Chicago, the grandfather of Handong's English service pastor, visited HGU. Young-Gil said to him, "Attorney Lee, won't you come and work with us at Handong?" From then on, Attorney S. K. Lee worked passionately to make the International Law School a reality. Finally, the Ministry of Education of Korea approved the Graduate School of Handong International Law School (HILS) in 2002, which is indeed the first American style Law school in Asia.

The chartered Dean of Handong International Law School, Lynn Buzzard, in class

"Do Justice, Love Mercy, and Walk Humbly With Your God" *(Micah 6:8).* Later, through the introduction of Pastor Billy Kim, the former Chairman of the Baptist World Alliance, Professor Lynn Buzzard, of Campbell University Law School in North Carolina was invited to be the chartered Dean of HILS. As an attorney and pastor,

he had worked not only with various U.S. law firms but also had advised governments of various Asian countries on their constitutions. He also founded the Christian Legal Society (CLS) in the United States, which impacted the legal environment in that country. What is amazing is that he had been praying for a law school that would produce Christian lawyers. HILS was the answer to his prayers. At the third admissions ceremony for HILS in 2004, Ambassador Thomas C. Hubbard, the then U.S. Ambassador to Korea, honored us with his presence. HILS attracted much interest and attention from education circles and international societies. As of 2006, students from over 18 countries are studying at HILS. HILS offers full scholarship to students from developing countries. In June 2005, five students from the first class of HILS who graduated in December 2004 passed the U.S. bar fort of the State of Tennessee and many followed the same afterwards. In 2006, additional 9 students passed the Bar Exams. If a dream is conceived, it is realized in due time.

Good News to All Nations!

One day, Young-Gil received a letter from a Handong graduate-missionary, who served in Sri Lanka.

Dear President Kim:

Living by faith in Sri Lanka is not easy. At first, I was filled with the Holy Spirit and lived well, but after a while, I was burnt out and the smile disappeared from my face. I asked God what brought me here.

Once with a Korean medical missionary team, I went to the northern Tamil area, a land of unimaginable poverty. Unable to find food, children ate sand and people waited in long queues to see doctors, whom they say they have not seen for the last 20 years. We could not take a break because people kept coming endlessly. In one corner, I saw some medical staff folding papers for the medicine. It was a simple labor that was repeated over and over again, but they were serving joyfully, without complaining.

Suddenly, tears streamed down on my face. I realized that they portrayed the image of the foreign missionaries who came to Korea a century ago and provided medical services to Koreans living in poor rural villages. Our ancestors probably could not understand a word of the foreign doctors, just like these Sri Lankans. That medical team probably left the Korean village without seeing any change in the people. Yet, the early missionaries to Korea continued serving the people, as they had not come to see people, but to serve God.

That was how the Gospel was spread in Korea, and as a result, we came to this distant land to return the love we had once received in 1880s. Suddenly, my heart was filled with God's compassion, and I could see my problem, my indifferent heart toward the local people. God was in their midst. God was working for them, and God had called me to reach them. I was once again challenged and became thankful that I was included in His plan for this country. I will now devote myself all the more to intercessory prayer for the country.

Her letter resembled that of Dr. Horace G. Underwood, who came to Korea 130 years ago from the United States to share the Gospel. Dr. Underwood's diary in 1885, reads:

Underwood's Prayer for Chosun (Korea)
"Oh Lord, No there is nothing here to see.

Lord, the arid and poor land.

This land doesn't even have one tree growing straight up.

This land is where you have planned for us to move.

It is a miracle that we were able to cross the wide Pacific Ocean.

This place is like you Lord was holding this land and put it away.

Now there is nothing to see.

Only thing I can see is the dark stubborn stained people.

They are dark, poor, tied up and conventional Chosun People.

And they do not even know why they are tied up.

They don't even know their pain.

If I try to take away their pain, their thought is distrust, and
    they are angry.

I cannot see the inside of the Chosun Man.

And the policy of this land is something I cannot see inside of.

If I never have a chance to see the women riding in the sedan
    chair,

What should I do?

I cannot see into the Chosun Mind.

I cannot see what it is I am supposed to do here.

But Lord I will obey you.

When I humbly obey, the Lord will start the work.

I believe the day will come they will be able to see with
their spirited eyes the work the Lord had done for them.

Leaning on your Words

"Now faith is being sure of what we hope for and certain of
what we do not see,"

I believe I will be able to see the faith future of the Chosen
People.

Now it is like I stand empty handed in a barren waste land.

Now they just point their fingers at me and call me the
white ghost.

But I understand their and our spirit wanting to be one.

And we know that we are one people under the Kingdom of
Heaven.

And we are all children of God.

This we know.

I believe the day will come that we can join by tears.

Now we don't have a church or school to worship in.

We are just here in the field watching with caution for
doubt of contempt.

But I believe it isn't too far for this land to be a land of mercy.

Lord please only hold onto my faith."

1885 Horace G. Underwood

Acts 29

In February 2005, we celebrated our seventh graduation ceremony. At each graduation, I think about my fears at the first admission ceremony of the school in the wilderness. I remember how the congratulatory plants fell, one by one, in the gusty wind and the fear as to how we were going to raise the children who were entering the school with great expectations. As new student in the school of the wilderness, I was like one of those plants. Now, 11 years later, God has led HGU to grow into a deeply rooted tree that will not shake no matter how strong the wind may be. He turned a school in the wilderness, filled with doubt and fear, into a place of faith and blessings.

At Handong's graduation ceremony, expression of gratitude and love overflowed, not easily witnessed at other universities. Students took off their cap before receiving their diplomas and bowed down on their knees on stage. All students lined up to bow in tandem to their parents and their professors. The valedictorian gave his remarks. After extending appreciation to all his mentors, parents, and friends, he said,

"There is one more person standing behind all of you, whom we should recognize. He has been praying for us all night long and is now here, soaked in His sweat. I saw Him standing here, watching us as we take our leave, full of emotions. Did you see Him too? He planned this school long before Handong was founded, and He led all of us to this place. He has fed us and clothed us with abundance. He is worthy to receive our very best, our most precious. He is Jesus Christ.

Handong's history is truly a story of tears. HGU was like a small child whose mother ran out of milk. Yet it has been able to stand before God and within our society, despite the numerous trials and persecutions, all because of God's amazing providence, grace, and touch. I introduced Him last because I hope that He will be remembered the longest when our ceremony ends today. What I learned at Handong is that a truly influential person is someone who is always honest before God and men. I will never forget this even in the midst of today's stark reality. We still have a long way to go, but I will never give up the dream to impact the world."

God guided this school of the wilderness in miraculous ways over the past 10 years, and He trained us as His disciples. And so, we call our school 'God's School' without any reservation. Our pains were great at times, but He has also given us wonderful gifts. Those gifts are the Handong students who wore their caps and gowns on graduation day. We are overjoyed when we receive the news that our graduates have been accepted by U.S. Ivy League universities, such as Harvard, Yale, and Columbia, to further their advanced studies. We feel rewarded when big name Korean companies praise the quality of our graduates.

Our hearts tremble as we imagine how these graduates will impact their nations, and we cannot wait to hear stories of how they serve as leaders and role models. Their potential is the true worth and joy that we experience everyday at this school of the wilderness. Chapter 29 of the Book of Acts continues here at Handong in the twenty-first century!

The Handong's history is indeed the pilgrim's progress, the realization of God's plan to spread the Gospel to the end of the remaining world. For the purpose, He chose a nameless debt-ridden, frail institution with a totally uncertain future rather than rich and famous universities which are easily found in the world - just as he chose to send Jesus, our savior, as a carpenter born on the manger in a stable.

This book is only the first volume of the Pilgrim's progress of Handong, and each new day of Handong is one more page written in the new volume that I cannot wait long to see. What we saw so far is only the tip of the iceberg of the God's grand plan for the school. God is steering the iceberg and when the whole plan is revealed, that should be the day when His message reaches the ends of the world and His Great Commission is fulfilled.

EPILOGUE:

My Husband Drives At Thirty-Five Miles Per Hour

*W*e were living in Troy, New York in 1972, and our son Ho-Min was just old enough to ride his tricycle. He used to ride a tricycle in front of our house, but now and then he would stop the tricycle all of a sudden and lie down on the ground looking up the sky. Then, he would get up again and kick the tricycle tire with his small foot and ride it again. He looked like he was checking to see if the tire was out of air. He would play this game whenever he rode his tricycle, and so one day, I asked him, "Why do you keep lying on the ground when you're playing with your tricycle?"

"Daddy lies down under the car, and so does Janet's daddy. And, Steve's daddy too. And then, they all kick the tires!"

I could not resist bursting into laughter. Toward the end of 1960, most Korean students, who had come to the United States to study, had old, used cars. Every weekend, the most popular scenes in front of every Korean student's houses at RPI dormitory were men fixing cars with open hoods, lying underneath the chassis. Most of them were engineering students, so they were handy and were able to fix most of the problems on their own. Jimmy Ho-Min, probably, had thought that a tricycle would only work if he did the same thing.

Since New York winters were almost always filled with snow, roads were usually salty to prevent the road from turning icy. Older cars were always covered with rust. Even so, the Korean students proudly drove their rusty and cranky old cars everywhere. Our car was relatively new compared with those of our neighbors. Young-Gil was quite proud that our blue car was a Dodge, and even a GT at that, and subtly but surely, emphasized the fact that it was a virtually "new," pre-owned car, that was only five years old.

That autumn in 1972, we left on our first trip since our wedding with five other Korean-student couples on a picnic to enjoy the fall colors. I prepared for the outing with excitement. Riding in Young-Gil's proud Dodge GT, we were on the road in a caravan with five other cars. It was about a two-hour drive from Troy, New York, to Bennington. As we drove through beautifully colored foliages, a sign appeared on the roadside that read "Speed Limit 35 Miles per Hour." Young-Gil slowed to a crawl. When cars began lining up behind us, he pulled our car over to the shoulder and signaled them to pass. Other cars passed by speedily, and the distance between our friends and us continued to widen. Soon, we could not see the last car ahead of us any more, but my husband insisted on driving at 35 miles an hour keeping the speed limit. I got more and more frus-trated and cried, "We'll lose our friends!"

Still, he did not speed up; he continued to drive at 35 miles an hour. Eventually, we came to a fork in the road. We hesitated for a moment, and ended up taking a wrong road. There were no cell phones at the time, and since we did not have a map with us, we could not find our friends no matter how far we drove. We returned home exhausted after driving all day long for nothing. I immedi-ately crawled into bed and pulled the blanket over my head in anger, 'Everyone else drove fast without any problems. What good was a Dodge GT? He shouldn't even brag about his car. How can I live my lifetime with someone who is so stubborn?'

I had been looking forward to the picnic so much. I was angry for having it ruined, and I resented my husband for it. Years later, I wondered, "Did God call Young-Gil to be the President of Handong because He knew that Young-Gil would not give up and stay at 35 miles an hour once he was on the road?" Young-Gil was accused unfairly and wrongfully, but he never once faltered. In contrast, how

I wished countless times that the reality we faced was a nightmare from which I would soon wake up!

Young-Gil still lives his life at 35 miles per hour. Insisting on Handong as the only path, he travels the road with undivided attention. If he had been the type of a man who was more flexible and worldly, one who calculated his profits and losses, he could not have stayed at Handong based on his promise to God alone. He would have quit when the founder gave up on the school before it opened and the school had no source of income, then or later. But God gave him the simplicity and steadfastness of a character that insisted on 35 miles per hour. And God allowed him to keep driving at that speed despite the unbearably difficult attacks, false accusations, and dire lack of funds.

Pastor Ha once remarked, "Two years ago, President Kim delivered a congratulatory speech for an elders' ordination ceremony at the church. But instead of saying 'church,' he accidentally said, 'All of you have been dedicated to serve Handong Global University.' The one who was sweating was Mrs. Kim, who was standing behind him on the stage. President Kim hadn't even realized what he'd said. Whenever I talk with President Kim, he doesn't talk about anything else. His topic is always about Handong. President Kim is obsessed with Handong and Handong only, the one mission that God has given him."

God has called Young-Gil to be His tool. Sometimes, I complain to my husband who has no interest in anything but the school. I tell him, "Your oral communication contains only subjects, verbs and objects, but when it comes to the story of Handong, your speech suddenly transforms to have many adjectives and adverbs."

Watching my husband from my vantage at his side, I realize again and again how profound the providence of God is. God used a man of slow speech as a lecturer on creationism as well as a witness of the Gospel, and He chose an unsociable scientist who was more familiar with research apparatus than people, to become a university president, a position that dealt with a thousand different types of people. He assigned a man, who never knew how much money he had in his wallet, to lead a financially strapped university and manage school finances that required tens of millions of dollars.

After such a choice, God took care of everything Himself, and I witnessed His work firsthand.

Young-Gil testifies, "God gives responsibility to those who are confident, but to an insufficient person like me, He takes all the responsibility Himself. If God used only perfect people, then there wouldn't be any work left in the Kingdom of God for someone like me to do. *"God is truly the Wonderful Counselor and Mighty God!" (Isaiah 9:6).*

"If I must, I will boast of the things that show my weakness" (II Corinthians 11:30).

Even today, there is a path at Handong on which we must travel, city walls that we must rebuild, and the youths of Handong like the morning dews, who will go forth to find the lost souls of God. Young-Gil firmly believes, even today, that God personally leads HGU, and he simply drives forward at 35 miles per hour on His behalf.

I know that he desires to become more like Jesus. I pray that one day when we stand before our Lord, having done the work on this earth as He has called upon us to do, the precious image of our Lord be found on my husband's face, having traveled through this world at 35 miles per hour. I look forward to the joy that we will share with our Lord then.

"I will praise the Lord all my life; I will sing praise to my God as long as I live" (Psalm 146:2).

THOUGHTS:

The Jerusalem of My Soul

The air inside the gates of Handong was different from the air outside. The moment I stepped inside the school entrance, I felt as if my soul was being immersed in the scent of peppermint. It was a mysterious scent. The students, the professors, even the grass -nothing seemed ordinary. Songs of heaven could almost be heard if you listened carefully enough. My heart trembled. Where did the excitement come from? Once, twice - every time I stepped into the campus, my heartbeat became clearer and stronger. I began to hear the knocking on my soul: the sound that was repairing the prayers that the world had shattered; the sound that was raising up the conscience that the world had shattered; the sound that was raising up the conscience that the world had shattered; the sound that was lifting up to heaven the love that the world had shattered! This place was a new world where spirits were lifted, where dreams painted the sky in full colors, where hope and courage grew in faith like oak trees.

God's abundant grace had rescued Korean people from the extreme poverty, but everything else was rotting away in our land where immorality, obscenity, and injustice ruled. Some things fall away without a sound, and some things fall away making roaring sounds that shake the earth, but our generation, which has branded its conscience with a hot iron, is wasting away without making any sound.

God had anxiously been looking for workers to rebuild the devastated walls of the spirit of Jerusalem in our land. God had sadly been looking at the fallen walls of Jerusalem on our land, and had been looking for His Nehemiah who would rebuild the walls. He was awaiting to hear the cries of Nehemiah, who wept at the news of the fall of Jerusalem's walls from our land.

Handong is a school that God founded to rebuild the fallen walls of the spirit of Jerusalem. He led a scientist who knew nothing of worldly ways to that place. His choice was a simple man who knew nothing of power, ambition, or money. God led this man, who had been living a life of comfort and security as a scientist, into the Red Sea of Pohang. And, just as He did to Nehemiah who staked his life on his prayers, He made this man pray with his life. This man had the humility of Nehemiah who knew the importance of partners, and had the courage to confront evil without fear. He did not hesitate when faced with risk. He did not sit in a leader's seat, but he worked in the forefront – he was a man of action who moved forward, resolute in his convictions.

President Young-Gil Kim did not consider his students to be his disciples. He did not think of his relationships with them as those of teacher and students. To him, his students were God's people who would transform the world, God's workers and his partners who would be with him in heaven. The students followed him – looking to him sometimes as their father, sometimes as their friend.

President Kim took his position at a school midst a serious financial crisis. He had no money from the very beginning. He was not only short on funds, but also surrounded by obstacles and adversaries that prevented him from managing the school. Every path led to a dead end. Those who loved Handong wondered with anxious hearts why things were turning out that way. Who was causing the eye of the storm? Why were others persecuting the school with such tenacity? The fact that Handong continued to exist on prayers without falling was a mighty miracle indeed. Handong walked on stepping-stones of miracles to be where it is today. Its history is one of persecution through countless accusations and trials. Such attacks were not merely isolated incidents – they formed an avalanche.

Handong was a Jerusalem that compelled me to reflect on my spirit. Handong was a sequel to the Book of Acts in our times. When I look upon the President, the professors and the students, I see the Lord who walked with them inside a blazing furnace. President Young-Gil Kim and Mrs. Young-Ae Kim are straightforward and simple average people who are exactly as they appear. It has been a blessing in faith for me to meet them. I cried over and over endlessly as I read the words that Mrs. Kim wrote in tears, sweat and blood, as she endured with her husband the incredible pains and afflictions that fell upon them in the name of God. The miracle that appeared through their pain was a true grace. The profound and mysterious ways of God's love were so amazing that I, too, had to kneel down on the stepping-stones of His love and cry. Sometimes, I cried out to God because I found my faith so shabby since what filled me inside contained nothing but trash. Other times, I cried because I felt so ashamed of the sordid state of my spirit in presence of His mighty providence. Only God would understand the beauty of President and Mrs. Kim, their record of professors and students who were their partners; the record that speaks of their willingness to forsake their lives of comfort, prestige, and security without regret for God's work. They did this believing that God had founded Handong, and they embraced the youths of Handong with their entire lives. These words are not the words of an individual. These words are a witness to the love and miracle of God who acts through trials and pain.

By Yun-Hee Chung (Chairman of the Association of
Korean Fiction Writers)

PAPYRUS BASKET

Do you remember the papyrus basket that housed Moses?
Handong Global University is like the Papyrus Basket.
As Moses - housed in the Papyrus Basket - was later used as
   God's man
to save the world's races (Exodus 2:3),
Handong students will be the future leaders who change the world.

Handong Global University as God's university, wants to be
   the Papyrus Basket
that produces God's people who will save all nations.
In the time when many feel desperate that there is little hope in
   this world,
We have hope because of Handong Global University
for we have God, the dream that He gave us and the precious
   students that He sent us.

In this world ill with ethical and spiritual decay,
we need prayers and participation of those who want God
and await for birth of GOD'S UNIVERSITY.
But the new history through Handong cannot be realized without
   your prayers and support.
Handong would like to invite you as our partners of Papyrus Basket.

Handong International Foundation (HIF) is a
tax-exempt non-profit organization under the tax code 501(c)(3)
with the following address:
HIF
c/o Rev. Jong-Yong Lee, Chairman of HIF
Cornerstone Church
24428 S. Vermont Avenue
Harbor City, California 90710
Tel : (310)530-4040
Fax : (310)530-8400
E-mail: lahandong@hotmail.com
Handong Global University: www.handong.edu